HARRY,
THE
RAT
WITH
WOMEN

HARRY, THE RAT WITH WOMEN

A NOVEL BY
JULES FEIFFER

PUBLISHED BY
FANTAGRAPHICS BOOKS

FANTAGRAPHICS BOOKS
7563 LAKE CITY WAY NE
SEATTLE, WASHINGTON 98115

EDITED BY GARY GROTH
DESIGN BY ADAM GRANO
COVER ILLUSTRATION BY ROGER LANGRIDGE
PROMOTION BY ERIC REYNOLDS
PROOFREAD BY GREG ZURA
PUBLISHED BY GARY GROTH AND KIM THOMPSON

Distributed in the U.S. by W.W. Norton and Company, Inc.
(212-354-500)

Distributed in Canada by Raincoast Books
(800-663-5714)

Distributed in the United Kingdom by Turnaround Distribution
(108-829-3009)

ISBN: 978-1-56097-793-3
First printing: March, 2007
Printed in Singapore

**FOR
JUDY**

CONTENTS:

THE
LOVE
OBJECT

HARRY,
THE
RAT
WITH
WOMEN

THE
LOVE
MONSTER

PART ONE

THE
LOVE
OBJECT

Pro″to-zo´a… A phylum of animals whose chief characteristics are that the body consists of only a single cell… and that they reproduce, not by eggs or spermatozoa, but by the fission of the body… into two or more new individuals Among them are the lowest and simplest of known animals, but some exhibit a considerable number of parts and organs…

— *Webster's New International Dictionary, Second Edition*

And the reason is that human nature was originally one and we were a whole, and the desire and pursuit of the whole is called love.

— Plato, *Symposium*

1.

Little Harry was loved; of that he was aware every waking hour of the day. But not even in sleep did love escape him. During the day his big, athletic-smelling father and his thickening, plum-ripe mother lavished him with the sweet fragrance of their affection. Their passion, their whole appetite was for Harry, *their* little Harry, who had come to them so late, so unexpectedly, so long after all hope for miracles was gone. But, unlike other parents who found their children lovable enough to eat — and so did — Harry's approached the object of their appetite with the innate sensitivity of born gourmets. They prepared him for dinner, but nibbled only lovingly and slightly, savoring the act, inhaling its aroma and noting it forever in their book of memories, and then ever so delicately pushing away from the table to gently demur another serving — "Tomorrow, maybe. Not now."

And in his sleep, love, a thing as real to him as his house or his bicycle, rolled with Harry in its arms, over and over, warm and slow; the woman: love. It never left him. He walked with it on the street to school and, at his desk, it gently proctored him when he needed to remember famous dates or the multiplication table. One day the teacher, who always called on Harry first (the divine right of personal magnetism), asked, "Harry, what does your father do?" Harry stood up at his desk and answered, "Love."

The class roared dirtily. The teacher flushed. "Love whom?" she bravely asked. And Harry answered, "Me."

This time the class did not stir; Harry was more certain of his father than any of them could be of theirs.

Harry could not avoid being loved. Physically he was the perfect child — expect no description here — everyone has his own image of perfection; Harry fit them all. He was only to be seen in soft focus with blurred, tear-filled eyes. "Wonderful," said the passing stranger, "like a painting." But he would not dare pinch a cheek or squeeze an arm or inflict the pain which is an adult's way of checking off perfection in a child — as if the only means to recognize it is to mar it. Harry's was the kind of beauty that set its own terms on admirers. They would not come close unless he allowed them.

He knew and accepted the fact that he was beautiful. Just as any prodigy looks upon his gifts as normal, because for him they are, Harry regarded his aptitude for beauty with equanimity; he saw nothing peculiar about it; since he felt very special why should he not look very special? Again, like the prodigy, he centered his focus on his aptitude, studying methods to enhance its development; practicing for hours out of the day before his mother's mirror the arts of facial expression and body movement. His taste about himself was impeccable; his drive was strong; to stay only this beautiful was sheer defeatism; to grow more beautiful with the years — now that was a goal a boy could work toward.

It was never noticed nor would it have seemed strange if it had been, that Harry thought only of himself. Since all those around him thought only of Harry, the boy was merely following example. His mirror was fine company; his toys were bores in comparison. Strangely, children were no more free of his spell than were their elders or Harry himself. Girls, dumbstruck in his presence, wrote his name on sheets of paper and pinned them close to their hearts where in their dreams they could speak to the paper and listen to its rustle beneath their dresses return their love. Boys became his functionaries, his retinue: they ran his errands, did his homework, and crowded as close to him as they dared, watching his wandering eye jealously to see which of them he favored as a best friend. But Harry's eye always wandered back to itself. His servitors knew no satisfaction, but only hunger and self-loathing for being unworthy; for being different. They saw Harry as the norm. The multitude beneath him were unfortunate aberrations shabbily highlighted by the glow of his perfection. Parents lost their pride in their children; seeing Harry made them feel toward their own the mixed emotions one feels toward an invalid. On the day Harry's mother took him on his only trip to the zoo, the animals could not take their eyes off him.

At an early age it became clear to his parents that Harry was going to be something special — a famous man, perhaps President, perhaps even a movie star. To prepare him for his destiny they saw he would require a special kind of training: a tutorship aimed at channeling his beauty in constructive directions. They had little means; his father was a physical education instructor in the city high school system, his mother was a private nurse. But relatives — aunts and uncles, cousins, nieces and nephews — insisted on raising a monthly Harry Fund as an investment; a premium on Harry's future. "Don't worry about it," they philosophized grandly. "Isn't he ours as much as yours? He'll pay us back."

With the first month's installment, a full-time tutor and governess was employed. Her name was Fanny Braintree.

At the time his tutorship began, Harry was still a quiet child; unresponsive to the demands of an adult world that placed a sliding scale of values on a child's cuteness or cleverness. Cuteness he had no need for, or cleverness either; both were defensive affectations designed to gain the attention that Harry by being Harry automatically had. His language from the beginning dealt only in basics; his first spoken word was "Harry," his first sentence was "Give me." His baby remarks were hardly quotable but they got for him all that he wanted. As he began to grow into boyhood, he saw no urgent need to amplify them; his beauty was in the eye, not the ear of the beholder. When, during an English lesson, he asked his public school teacher, "What good is all this stuff going to do me?," she could honestly offer no answer. In terms of formal education he had fallen far behind; yet, in some ways, not very far behind Fanny Braintree.

Miss Braintree was in mid-passage when she came to tutor Harry. She was, by nature, a large, voluptuous woman and, by principle, a slender, shapeless one. Feeling heavily the *responsibility* of a career in education, she entered the field by dieting most of her shape away and then tightly corseting whatever she found left. Through such sanctification she placed her own soul in readiness for those tiny little other souls whose future and guidance lay helpless in her hands. Her male friendships had been restricted to several YMCA secretaries with whom she read poetry. For years she had not stared at a man below the first button on his suit.

But now she was on her way elsewhere: quietly and mysteriously her direction had changed; the layers of protection had cracked; her corsets no longer fit; her body was rather tentatively bursting through. Her mind was suddenly awake to hidden possibilities and her attempts to keep them hidden were half-hearted and, so, failed. Secretly, she entertained dreams and engaged in forbidden practices. At age forty Miss Braintree had discovered adolescence. Shortly thereafter she discovered Harry.

One popular dream of youth is to have had a sultry seductress of a governess who pads into one's bedchamber on nights the grownups are away at the opera, warmly sheds her paltry negligee and slips beneath the covers to teach one those facts she fears might otherwise be picked up in the streets.

If Fanny Braintree was not of that calibre, her dreams were. She came to love Harry madly but, being raised in a tradition where a young woman was only aggressive about those things she didn't want, she demurely and passively waited for the object of her love, just turned eleven, to pad silently into *her* bedchamber, fold her into his arms and stretch open those doors which, at all other times, she had to open for herself. Though during tutoring sessions the Harry of her dreams never once conflicted with the little boy she tutored (a woman never makes the first move), at night the other Harry, *her* Harry, subverted and confused her senses. He was no age and no shape. He was Man!

And since he never *did* show up, though night after night she left her door across the hall just a bit ajar and posed a bottle of sherry with two empty glasses on her bedtable, she came to resent him for his boorishness; she came to hate him. That dirty, teasing, frustrating rat of a Harry!

Eventually, Miss Braintree's odd evening habits came to the attention of Harry's family. Each night there were two empty glasses and a full bottle of sherry at her bedside; each morning there was an empty bottle of sherry and two ruby-stained glasses in their place. An odor, other than love, began to fill the household.

Fanny Braintree was a controlled and practiced tutor of the old school; her ability to communicate thickened slightly but never fogged. Her lessons were given in a loud, almost overly clear voice and only during written examinations, while Harry's face was buried busily in a test paper, did her pink-rimmed eyes and her sagging chalked face gaze at him in fond regret;

all love at the sight of him; all womanly forgiveness at her wretched lover's lack of faith. She soon took to writing poems which she tied with rubber bands around small rocks and left in Harry's path as he strolled in the garden. Harry never read unless he had to, so he ignored the poems. At night, as the family sat singing 'round the piano, she'd sneak back among the bushes and nervously recover her scattered rocks.

Harry's parents became disturbed. "The wine glasses, the open door, the moping around the garden. What does it all mean?" the mother asked. "Let's be patient a little longer," replied the father in self-interest. That night, on their way to bed as they passed Fanny Braintree's open door, Harry's father knew he must quickly arrive at a decision. He had known for weeks what the poor bedeviled tutor must be going through: her romantic dream of love, the waiting wine glasses, the inviting door, the lost walks in the garden lamenting a frustration she could barely control. No woman had ever wanted him this way and though Fanny Braintree did not have the spare, gymnast's type of build he found attractive, he felt himself thinking of her with a growing excitement. How long could he resist the adventure? Was it fair to Fanny Braintree to let her wither? Was it fair to Harry — wouldn't it adversely affect his lessons? He could scarcely believe his wife would mind if she but understood the purity of his motives; the rehabilitation aspects of his projected program.

The night-after-night passing of that open door slowly maddened him. He stirred in his sleep, drank warm milk, fought desperately against the growing image of that tantalizing enchantress with the golden body whose arms waited to welcome him the moment he chose to cross her portal. But this was not the way to go to her; it was unclean. It was guilty. He had to establish control over his emotions, see her again as a poor bereft woman and himself as a minister to her needs.

One night, after long and thoughtful drinking, he at last felt the keen blue blaze in his heart flamboyantly signaling the purity he had sought. He took off his scuffs, tiptoed up the stairs and, with passion mixed with a sense of social work (he *was* a phys ed instructor), he slipped into Miss Braintree's room.

Could it be happening at last? These strong arms holding her? This fine body smelling of the gymnasium and the turkish bath crushing her beneath its insistent weight? This dark room with *his* dark shape? How could it be? *Could* it be? "Harry," she groaned ecstatically. "Oh my dearest Harry."

"Who's this Harry?" came back a voice. "Don't talk so loud or you'll wake up my wife."

Her screams did.

It became clear that Miss Braintree had to go. She left early on a cold, rainy morning without saying goodbye to Harry or to anybody. In her baggage was a purloined cameo of her love — a childhood cameo to be sure — but nevertheless a memento of those glorious nights spent waiting for the moment that the door opened wide, the sherry was poured and the sweet wine taste decantered into her own true love's lips. Nothing else was real to her. Everything else was forgotten.

Years later, her juices dry and living sadly, she would hear of Harry's exploits and smile to herself — "That beautiful rat. I taught him everything he knows. I hope he remembers me kindly."

At an emergency meeting of the Harry Fund it was decided that it did not serve the purposes of that organization for its monies to be diverted into a procuring fee for inconstant husbands. It was further decided best for Harry's future that the Fund's trustees take over the management of his education. Though his mother and father had patched up their differences, they were in too much of a state of shock to argue with the decision. Harry was sent off to Europe in the ripening hands of his nineteen-year-old cousin, Gloria. It was hoped that he would receive a classical education.

2.

Gloria was not beautiful actually, but she was terribly sexy. Everybody thought so. She was sexy in the way only girls in their teens, physically innocent and mentally dirty, can be. No woman with real knowledge would have dared move with that semi-practiced invitational sway. It was strictly a way of walking for the young and once the sex line was crossed the young walked differently too. Once carnal, twice shy.

Gloria was uneasy about her feelings for her cousin Harry. She was, of course, feverishly in love with him; an emotion she found convenient to interpret as big-sisterly affection. Pigeon-holed thusly, she could allow herself to sit by the side of his bed each night and stroke his hand, brush back his hair and whisper to him as he dozed, "I feel just like a sister to you. Just like a sister."

But although she could control her feelings *for* Harry, she was far less able to control her feelings *against* him. Aboard ship *he* was the one getting all the attention! He stole her sense of burgeoning beauty and there was nothing to do but hate him for it. And the tiring reverberations of her hate bouncing against her love brought forth a groan of futile anger. Why wasn't Harry as wound up with her as she was with him?

To have admitted any of this would have meant adding a real sin to her extensive list of imagined ones. So she traded insight for bitchiness and gained immeasurably by the exchange. She collared all the young men on board and proceeded to drive them mad with accidental intimacies. Some she brought back to their cabin so that Harry, asleep, could be wakened by the laughter, the squeals, the outraged slaps, and the revoked promises in the next stateroom. Gloria had few natural charms but her instincts were excellent. Her victims complained but submitted, using their wider range of experience to assure themselves that during their remaining five days at sea they would surely bring her around. She was, they thought, a young goofy kid, and tomorrow would be another day. They accepted her provocation and waited patiently for their revenge. By the fourth day out no attractive man under thirty was able to walk upright.

It was an education for Harry. At first he tried to blot out the teasing in the next room and get back to sleep but soon he began to listen to it as a form of theatrical entertainment. It became a favorite play for him. Each night there was a minor change of cast (the male's role), but the lines were about the same and the situations were identical.

"Stop! That tickles," Gloria would begin.

"It didn't tickle on deck."

"I mean it."

"Sure you do." (pause)

"Boy, you *are* fresh."

"Bet your life I am." (longer pause and sound of scuffling)

"Jeepers, you're clumsy."

"Yeah?" (continued scuffling)

"Do you want me to do it for you?"

"*I'll* do it."

"Jeepers, you really take a night and a day. It's only a simple hook."

"Yeah?" (pause — heavy breathing)

"I don't want to any more."

"What do you mean?"

"It's not romantic now."

"What do you mean?"

"I don't know. You make it seem like manual *labor* or something."

"What's the matter?"

"Do you have to lean on me that way?"

"C'mon."

"You're too persistent. I'm not in the mood any more."

"Well for Christsakes get back in the mood."

"Quiet! My little cousin's asleep in the next room."

"Listen, don't try to give me what you give other guys!"

"Are you so different from other 'guys'?"

"I'm *me!*"

"You're cute."

"Yeah?" (pause)

"Not now, I told you."

"When?"

"I'm tired now."

"When?"

"I'll see."

"That's a promise now."

"I'll see."

"See you in the morning?"

"I'll see."

Harry was less interested in Gloria, who bored him (he could not understand what all the fuss was about), than he was in the obviously victimized men. He had never heard voices so uniformly strained, so defenseless, so pleading; even during their moments of outburst and accusation he could hear their intimidated whine. It seemed so silly. It wasn't a matter of what they wanted, it was that anyone could so much want *anything* outside himself that puzzled him. Ridiculous!

During the early evening hours when Gloria left him alone to go vamping, Harry took to playing sexual conquest with himself in front of the mirror. He whined at himself with the men's lines and rejected himself with Gloria's. Then he laughed like anything. He felt beyond the game and so quickly grew bored with it. He understood that the men wanted some kind of love and that Gloria teased them about getting it. But he couldn't see why anyone had to run after love that way. What good was it if you had to chase it or be made to feel silly by it? He felt he knew so much more than these grown men. "Don't be so dopey," he wanted to say to them. "Don't go to them. Let them come to you!"

Harry smiled with this superior knowledge all the rest of the way to Le Havre. Gloria was sure that it was she the smiles were aimed at. He was laughing at her! Her week of hard work was wasted. She was being patronized! Bitterly she reflected that there could be no further doubt about it: her cousin Harry was a little rat. Well, let him go to hell. She was going to Paris.

"Paris," she said to herself, "Paris." And suddenly she realized that it meant no more to her than if she had said "Bronx." The scent of Paris had become overripe; the scent of sex took on the smell of cheese. Gone were her intricately detailed fantasies: her invented seduction, her invented violence, her invented pain. Gone, also, was her invented guilt. She saw the senselessness of her chaste triumphs; what point was there in evading that final experience, knowing, as she now did, that there could be no pleasure in it? Since it couldn't be fun, why not try it? She stared at Harry's smile and smiled ambitiously back. They would be landing soon and she would have to make plans. There could be no further doubt about it: let cousin Harry go to Paris; *she* was going to hell.

It wasn't until four years later that Harry surrendered his virginity — just three years and eleven months past the day that Gloria abandoned hers. He was still touring the continent with his cousin and quite content at being celibate even though fifteen, a thought unbearable to most of his contemporaries. "That stuff is stupid," Harry instructed them.

"Still and all," said a friend, "I'd sure like to tear off a piece of *that*," and he pointed to a particularly striking young lady striding handsomely down the Via Veneto.

"It shouldn't be too difficult," said Harry. "Just ask her. How do you know she won't say 'yes'?"

His two friends laughed nervously.

"I mean it," insisted Harry.

Their nervousness increased. "Let's go to a cinema," said one.

"Signorina," called Harry.

The woman turned with a half smile to stare at the amusing children she knew were following her. If she found them charming she would buy them each a piece of candy.

Harry smiled warmly. "My friends and I wondered if we could make love to you. All right?"

"Of course," the woman answered dazedly. Harry's friends ran.

3.

Harry returned to America at seventeen and sat around the house. He was in the least interesting phase for a person whose single concern was self-indulgence; that phase where the child may or may not be father to the man and all one can do is stick around to find out.

When he looked at the world he saw nothing that he wanted; when he looked at himself he saw that though everything was there, he still wanted more. He wanted a direction.

"Harry, what would you like to do?" the Harry Fund asked him.

"Who knows?" said Harry, annoyed at being asked to consider the question.

"Would you like to go into business?"

"Are you kidding?" said Harry.

"Would you like to go into law?"

"Christ!" said Harry.

"Would you like to be a doctor?"

Harry left the room in disgust.

The Harry Fund went into emergency sessions. After a night and day of debate it was decided that their protégé should be sent to college.

"College! Some direction," sulked Harry. But when he was promised a new wardrobe he agreed to go.

Last to hear of the decision were his parents. The Fund's lawyer sent them a registered letter telling them of the plan. They were ecstatic and, in keeping with their nightly habit, cried themselves to sleep — this time out of joy.

Harry's father had grieved himself into poor health and retirement over the sin hanging heavy in everyone's heart but his own these past years. His conscience was clear but he had too much pride to defend himself before a jury of familial peers. He would die first, he — at one time defiantly and later wistfully — told himself, and it was a probability that loomed more real by the day. His wife remained loyally by his side, the hapless helpmate of the haplessly convicted. The la-de-da with Fanny Braintree had become as much her crime as her husband's — no, even more her crime because somehow, in some way, it was her failure. The incessant devotion she had given her son had forced her husband to lust elsewhere than the marital bed. Over and over she kept telling her husband, "I'm sorry, I'm sorry," and he forever answered back, "I forgive you. I forgive you."

It was a more beautiful love than either of them had ever known and it was killing them both. The return of their son would have saved them, there could be no doubt of it, but they felt unworthy of owning him. The family had made a decision and, while they felt it was overly harsh in some ways, Harry's parents never dreamed of defying it. Theirs was a strong family tradition and family law was to be respected with a firmer rigidity than federal law, which, after all, was made up by strangers. "It's only right to abide by them," counseled Harry's mother. "Who helps us when we're sick?"

So the decision was unanimous.

"He'll get an education and find himself," said his parents. "He'll make contacts and find himself," said the trustees of the Harry Fund.

It soon became depressingly clear that his advisers were wrong. College was *awful*. Why were those stupid teachers talking about all those unimportant things when they should be talking about Harry? It didn't make him angry, it just left him puzzled at the odd mixture of meaningless values that seemed to control society. He managed not to hear a thing in class. He withdrew, disconnecting his hearing and turning all his sights inward. If life, all life, seemed to be as pointless as now seemed evident then he had to return to himself, work exclusively on himself and let outside interests go hang. He concentrated on his appearance, realizing that he was past the point where prettiness should have been left behind and animal virility added to his character. Since he despised athletics as needless sweat (any discharge from his body was viewed with grave misgiving) Harry found a considerable amount of self-absorption necessary to indulge himself into muscularness. But once successful, his mood of indecisiveness returned. Where was he to go? What was he to do? What he needed were answers!

"I just can't decide what to do with myself," he complained in class one day. The rest of the hour was spent in a discussion of his problem.

In his agitated state his magnetism operated erratically. Students and teachers bounced toward him and away like pellets caught in the spray of a geyser. Harry created no feeling, just suction and exhaust. His intake, when operating, swallowed the campus whole. He was elected president of fraternities to which he hadn't pledged; he was elected president of sororities who cared not a bit about details, they *wanted* him; he was given loving grades by instructors, the names of whose courses he had barely mastered.

And his exhaust was no less compulsive, sending a frigid chill of rejection across campus, leaving the school empty, spent and useless.

While at one time or another everyone on campus tried to get close to Harry, the only person who diverted his attention in the slightest was Dr. McCandless, his Science Fiction 1 professor, a white-haired, nervous man whose body was yellowed with nicotine stains and whose suits were marked with a powdery patina of ash which left cloud traces in the air whenever he moved. Harry found him curious because his interests were obviously as self-contained as his own.

McCandless believed and disbelieved everything, an attitude he considered most civilized. His nervously moving eyes wandered about his head as if on tiptoe, probing souls, asking questions, mocking authority and, at all times, displaying total lack of faith in whatever the mouth beneath it was saying. He delighted in self-contradiction, claimed individualism for his philosophy, and conspiracy for his passion. Single-handed, he had managed to organize a discontented underground of faculty who called themselves the Normalists and had as their motto "Those who *can*, teach."

Its membership varied depending on the time of year. Each fall, as students came out for football, the faculty came out for rebellion. McCandless grabbed the overflow from the socialists and the peace movement and formed a quorum. His dream was of revolution. Once a week he met with his co-conspirators and planned ways of perfecting society by eliminating it. But fall languished into winter and the conspiracy got bogged down in detail. The Normalists split into hard-liners and soft-liners. Theoretical differences divided the Senecalist Normalists from the Formalist Normalists. Rival factions denounced each other and withdrew from what they bitterly described as "politics." McCandless's desk became cluttered with theoretical explanations of abandonment which he brushed hurriedly away at the first sound of approaching footfalls. The conspiratorial slam of desk drawers rang day and night through the faculty building's corridors.

At the close of the school year McCandless would face the pathetic remains of his rebellion, wish them fraternal good wishes for a happy summer abroad, and devoutly promise a revived revolution for the fall semester. He spent his own summers indoors, at work on a series of state papers, a red phone always by his right hand in case he should be suddenly summoned to power.

But power shied away from him and he finally recognized that he was looked upon as a crank; his truths were too unpalatable. He understood the values of the marketplace; the only way to sell an unpalatable product was to present it in a form that seemed pleasant. McCandless admitted that the basic weakness of his revolution was himself. He just wasn't pleasant enough. His problem was to find an attractive leader — someone whose appearance and charm ably disguised the validity of the words he was speaking. McCandless would be the kingmaker — his need was for a king, an embryo Alexander to whom he would be the teacher, Aristotle. He smiled with a beam of commercial brilliance — what better choice than Harry?

Harry's possibilities were infinite! Who could resist the rhetoric of McCandless if it issued from the mouth of that boy? Clearly, no one. Yet it was a dangerous choice; McCandless was no less immune to Harry's spell than anyone else and during their moments together found his schemes drained away in a flood of affection and guilt. Such unreconstructed sentimentalism was not to be tolerated! He decided that he would have to avoid Harry in public. He chose, instead, to work through the mails.

One morning Harry received a letter addressed to "Occupant, Men's Dormitory, Room 1." The short note read: "Archetypal man wallows in apathy because he has ceased to care. Burn this letter!" The return address on

the envelope said Bon-Ami Soap Company. During the next five d
was a new letter every morning.

The second one read, "Archetypal man has ceased to care because he
has become alienated from himself. Think it over!" Harry didn't bother.
Certainly he felt alienated but he considered it a private problem; he hadn't
realized it was something that was going around. Annoyed at the prospect
that everyone had what he had, he ignored the third letter all of the next
day. Finally his curiosity got the better of him. What in the world was the
Bon-Ami Soap Company up to?

"Archetypal man," began the third letter, "has become alienated from
himself because he no longer controls the end product with which he
deals." Something in Harry quietly responded. What were the letters trying to tell him? The end product with which he dealt was himself. Had he
lost control? He waited for the fourth letter, expecting the answer.

"History bears witness that survival can come to archetypal man only
when he ceases to perfect the instruments by which he organizes society
and retools his skills to the perfection of *himself* !"

Harry was deeply moved. He reread the letters and burned them as instructed, saving only the supplemental reading lists included with each mail-
ing. Someday, he promised himself, he would have to get to the library.

McCandless decided that there was nothing further to be gained
through the mails; the time had come for a direct confrontation. He
planned it carefully, for if Harry were to be in the vanguard of the conspiracy it was essential to convert him at their first encounter. In that case,
it was best that the meeting take place at night — in the dark, so that the
conversion that took place was Harry's and not his own. In his last message he wrote: "Words mean nothing! The times call for action! Meet me
at midnight in the men's solarium." At the bottom of the note he could not

resist adding a short quiz.

"Cigarette?" offered McCandless in the sweat-smelling, smoke-smelling darkness.

"God, it smells in here!" said Harry. "I can hardly breathe with all these fumes."

"In a better society I wouldn't be this nervous and have to smoke," said McCandless, lighting and killing cigarettes.

"I didn't come here for that," grumbled Harry. "I need a direction."

McCandless splashed ashes excitedly. "I will be your direction and *you* will be the direction for millions of others!" All Harry could see of him were his yellow teeth glowing faintly in the blackness.

"Archetypal man" he began, using the phrase lovingly, "is now small because he has come to see himself as small. The Copernican revolution was an egregious error! Who but man should be the center of the universe? When man ceases to see himself as the center, he ceases to exist!"

"Everybody knows that," complained Harry. "What's that got to do with me?"

"The more man has centralized his society, that much more has he decentralized *himself*. Man has stopped seeing himself as *man*: he now sees himself as *mass-man!*"

"I don't care about other people," said Harry impatiently.

"I know what you're thinking," snapped McCandless, "you're thinking, 'But is man interested in his own perfection? Or is he only interested in his comforts?'

"I must answer regretfully that man *is* only interested in his comforts.

"'But do not his comforts alienate man from himself?' I can then hear you ask me.

"'Assuredly,' I would answer, 'and that is why we must take away his comforts.'

"'But is not man also interested in his machines?' you then ask.

"And my answer will be, 'Yes. And so we take away his machines.'

"'But then,' you continue, 'he will focus his attention on his children.'

"'That is true,' I answer. 'We will confiscate his children.'"

"The thing is — " Harry began.

But McCandless went on quickly. "'But then,' you protest, 'he will only divert his attention to his wife.'

"'We will remove her,' is my answer.

"'But then he will have no one to pay attention to!'

"'He will have himself,' will be my reply."

"Myself," murmured Harry in the smoky darkness.

"Only when the fifty states have seceded from the Union and the cities have seceded from the states and the villages from the cities and the neighborhoods from the villages and the families from the neighborhoods and the families themselves split like the atom into individual units — only when the chains of authority are broken everywhere so that even if we would, we could not put together an automobile, a television set, a happy family — only then will man, finding that he can not lose himself in the trivia of the outer world, return to where he belongs. And at that point he will cease to be alienated." McCandless paused for emphasis. "Only when *all* men cease to be alienated can one man return to himself."

Harry said nothing.

"For is it not true," continued McCandless, "that no man is an island while other men cannot also be islands? You can but answer 'yes.'"

"Yes," answered Harry in the dark.

4.

Resolved: that men are not sheep — this was to be the subject of the debate. McCandless set the theme, chose Harry as his non-sheep champion and, just to set the scales correctly, chose one of his underground compatriots, a stutterer, to resolve that men are. It would be a small trial, a test beginning of Harry's potential as a political leader. If all went well, then McCandless would write new speeches for him, eloquent testaments to the principles of Normalism. How the crowds would roar! (Rise to your perfectability, O man! Cast out your leaders! There are no dreams that cannot be made to come true!) McCandless heard it all as in a recorded playback.

And now Harry, too, was involved. The perfectability of man, yes, that could really be something. It was a theme with scope enough to tickle his insides and give him a warmth and excitement he had not felt for months. The perfectability of man — golly, what a concept — the perfectability of himself! Yes, here he was, Harry — the first perfect man, the proof that it could be done. He stared at himself in the mirror as if it were old times. God, politics was interesting.

Not surprisingly, the debate drew a mob. On the days preceding its occurrence, Harry walked around in a purple dream of self-involvement. The campus grew giddy in admiration and his path was followed by an army of love-sick admirers. They filled the hall. Seats had to be set up on the stage. Loudspeakers had to be set up outside the hall. No one could remember having heard of a more interesting, more fascinating, more vital topic than — Resolved: that men are not sheep. When Harry rose to begin the debate and announced in ringing tones of self-discovery — "Men are not sheep!" there was applause for fifteen minutes and several students wept with commitment.

It was a revelation to Harry. He had never tested his powers in this manner, was still not truly aware of what exactly his powers were. He never had the inclination to notice the passions others held for him. One only notices what is important; other people were never important.

"You can be perfected!" cried Harry. Once more there was wild applause.

"Cynics tell us that the common people — that's you, my friend, *and you*, and you, sir, and you too — yes, you, too, madam. Cynics tell us that the common people are easily controlled, that they believe the self-serving lies printed in the public, but not so free, press. Cynics say that the common man is corrupted and corruptible, interested in only his own and willing to go to war, to death, to suicide, the moment his government announces a new crisis to send him there. Do you believe that?" (chorus of angry Nooooooooo's)

"Well, you know what I say? I say Mr. Cynic is wrong, dead wrong! (applause: twenty minutes) I say that there's something in every man, no matter how lied-to he is, no matter how beaten down he is, no matter how used, abused, *confused* and misused he is (applause and laughter: five minutes), I say there's something — I don't know what to call it — maybe dignity — yes, dignity, an innate sense of striving toward the perfection of himself and his loved ones like a flower yearns for the sun — a need for truth as if it were a thirst — a need to throw out the captors, the crooks, the punks and the bunko artists — a need for the common man to be a man! And I say I'm all for that need!"

(applause: one hour and a half)

It took over three hours for Harry to complete his speech. At its conclusion his debating opponent threw his arms around him and, with tears cascading down his cheeks, hysterically conceded. McCandless danced crazily up and down in the wings. Billows of ash swept the air about him. Who could have believed it? A miracle! Who could have hoped for it? A miracle! He read the light in the audience's eyes as the reflection of the light in his own: the burning torch of Normalism! History was being made!

But to Harry it was as if he were lifted high and then suddenly dropped by a wave. He could not believe it was over. He basked in the love flowing toward him; it cleansed his body of layers of apathy and months of dullness. But it was over. He could not let it disappear so suddenly — not now, not when he had just discovered it. He raised his hand for silence. There was silence.

"I feel that if a debate has been announced a debate should take place. If it's O.K. with you I will now take the opposing position." The audience cheered. McCandless, registering a deep inner horror, found himself cheering too.

"Have any nation's citizens ever heard the call to arms and stayed home? Name me a war that has not been supported, name a crusade which, while it was winning, was not popular with the masses! Sheep? You are hardly even sheep. What sheep will not shy from danger but instead graze contentedly in a field surrounded by wolves? And yet there are wolves all around *you* and *you* graze! No, you are not sheep, you are grass! Green at the tip where it looks good. And brown and muddy at the root, passively waiting to be chewed and waiting on leaders to come decide for you when you've been chewed enough and when it's time to switch from one set of jaws chewing you to a *different* set of jaws! Grass will go in any direction it is blown. You are grass!"

"We're grass!" screamed the mob, writhing in self-flagellation. "Grass! Grass!!" the audience quivered in ecstatic release. "Muddy at the root! Muddy! Muddy! Muddy!" Women fainted. Faculty and students fell rolling on the floor, crawling as flat as possible; the closer to come to the new truth. McCandless wept and clawed the ground senselessly. "Why didn't I *think* of it? We're grass! We're grass!"

Harry viewed his work with growing detachment. Now that it was over he could see that it had nothing to do with him. He saw the crowd's frenzied devotion for what it was: a basically private release. Well, weren't they having a fine old time. He felt no further joy, just a growing sour distaste. "O.K.," he called out, "you're acting stupid. Everybody go home!" The audience rose, straightened its clothes and left. No, Harry decided, politics had no answers to offer him. It was too directionless a direction.

A week later, on the day that Harry left college for his parents' funeral, McCandless was putting the finishing touches on the constitution for his New Grass Roots Conspiracy.

5.

The funeral was treated by the family as if they had other things on their mind; which they did. Harry's parents had been dying slowly and undemandingly for years. The Harry Fund found their blamelessness terribly annoying. A family sticks together because of its problems. If members fail to pitch in and create problems it can only be analyzed as a subtle attack on the family's reason for being, a devious attempt to dissolve the ties. Well, nobody likes a troublemaker.

Their death was less a sudden going than a prolonged sinking into the earth, less a collapse than a disappearance beyond the horizon like the sun in a filmed travelogue. They went down warmly and bravely, blaming no one, loving everyone and thinking only of their son, Harry. They sank out of sight, the mother going first, the father following moments later because he was several inches taller.

Harry could not believe they were dead. He still sensed the presence of their love filling the air about him, their willing natures blending peacefully with his desires. He still felt that the world was as it had been. How could he know real grief when he was sure that they were not altogether dead? Perhaps people died in parts. But the part of his parents that had died

Harry had seen almost nothing of in seven years; the part that would never die, their ever-present gift of love, was with him as strong as ever. This part was still closest to Harry, supporting him in his anguish; the other part, the dead part, had given up, quit on him. He almost had contempt for it. Besides, there was other bad news to think about.

Hard times had come upon the trustees of the Harry Fund. Emergency expenses had depleted its coffers dangerously. The villain, it seemed, was his cousin Gloria, who had been subject to a recurring medical problem every six months or so for the last three years. The expense of transportation to Sweden and hospital costs had laid the family financially low. Harry was told that the best that now could be done for him was a few hundred every month. He would have to fend for himself.

He began to feel as if a ruthless, nasty game were being forced upon him. He had no intention of accepting the sort of world he was being squeezed into. Rarely did he show temper but now, for weeks on end, he was furious; and there was reason to be. He'd been cheated! The Harry Fund had promised him a career. Where was it? A direction — where was it? He had accepted them on good faith, let them serve and be loyal to him and now what was his thanks? Desertion. He didn't question that they loved him but there was efficient love and inept love. There was no doubt into which category theirs fell. He took the Fund's payment with an impatient gesture and went off to find a demoralizing, rat-infested room in a dirty, cheap rooming house. Two could play at their game.

The rooming house of his dreams was in a factory district where plant mechanization had been so perfected that no skilled labor was needed at all. The unskilled labor was largely recruited from the South, from sections rich with a lack of skills. The migrants lived drearily in tenements and rooming houses which spawned grubbily around the several factories. Everybody had dreams of doing something else. It would have been a neighborhood ripe for crime if, after a day's work, somebody had enough energy to commit one.

Harry was the only tenant in his rooming house who didn't work in a factory. Regardless of how bad his affairs went he would not reduce himself to taking a job. Work he understood as a convenient time-killing device in which people indulged themselves to avoid concentrating on the important thing: himself. It riled Harry to know how much activity took place in the course of a day that did not center on him. However, this would be an easy matter to set right. All he need do was acquaint himself with his neighbors and allow them to create a supplemental Harry Fund. The idea brightened his day and that night he stepped across the hall and knocked on the nearest door to begin making friends.

He made only one friend. Her name was Rosalie Murchison from Macon — or, as she said it (not as a name, but as a lyric) "RosalieMurchi sonFrom*Macon?*" It was RosalieMurchisonFrom*Macon?* who breathlessly opened the nearest door across the hall the instant Harry knocked, for who could tell — he might have been a Hollywood agent.

She was a temporary factory worker hopefully bound for glory in the film colony — if only she could get there. Beneath a splendid milky display of hair there spread, in a variety of directions, a baby-beautiful movie star's face and a super-womanly movie star's figure; as if she were not born of a piece but put together in a composite of bests by the underweaned editors of a girlie magazine. She looked too much larger than life for men to run after. Instead they told dirty jokes about her and claimed to have taken her to bed; the more nervous the man, the more graphic the claim. But no one had touched her. She wouldn't allow it. She was afraid of what uncontrolled handling would do to her skin tone.

RosalieMurchisonFrom*Macon?* was headed out to Hollywood to make the grand try. By careful saving and hard work she had put away $2500. In another six months she'd have $500 more; enough for a one-way bus ticket and a year's expenses. It was this thought that kept her going. Each new day of indignity heightened her removal by putting her that much closer to her dream — and made her seem cold and aloof for not hearing the remarks called after her by the wistful men on the line. Why should she when she wasn't even there? She was in the movies — protected in the arms of Robert Mitchum, who was saying, "To hell with 'em all, honey. You've got Burt Lancaster, Rock Hudson, and me."

Her real life was in her room. It was tattooed with glossy grinning photos of movie faces: great women stars, great men stars, and a wall full of anonymous almost — stars who had appeared in but one picture, where they were invariably listed after the rest of the cast following the words "And Introducing — " and were never after seen again.

But which of the winking, grinning faces on her wall could compare with Harry? He stood in the hall, smiling down at her, his words beating against her like bird's wings.

"I know it's short notice but I am strapped, so whatever you can give me I'd appreciate. Every little bit helps."

And then, through the use of what power she knew not, he was with her in her room, talking pleasantly, accepting her as an equal — "Well, I don't see any need to apologize. I'd say that twenty-five dollars is a swell beginning. Really, don't worry about it."

"It's enough? You sure now? You're not just being nice?"

"Who lives upstairs? Maybe they have more," he said, rising.

She blocked the door. There was no telling *who* lived upstairs.

"I have more! In the bank. Ever so much more. Honest to sweet

Saturday night, you have got to believe me!"

"I hate to be caught short," said Harry.

"Tomorrow. I'll go to the bank tomorrow."

How could he be unaware of the ground swells, unaware of the imbalance in the room, unaware that RosalieMurchisonFrom*Macon?*, who never doubted the splendor of her own appearance, now saw herself as fat and clubby and asked only to die for him? He needed money? He would have money!

She took him to dinner, she bought him gifts and clothes and tickets to the movies. They went to the movies endlessly and where the romance on the screen ended and the romance with Harry began blurred into meaninglessness. There was no difference, really. They were two heads forty feet high, meeting in the center of a giant screen, kissing stereophonically and fading out to the next scene, which was the same as the one just passed, repeated over and over. But it was a movie that never got anywhere. Rosalie MurchisonFrom*Macon?*, with the dwindling bank balance, began stirring restlessly in her seat wondering when the plot would start moving. She felt caves opening within her and they remained unfilled. Her skin began to dry and crack. Her juices were being drained — Harry was doing this to her.

"I can't believe it's real. Can you? I can't. I really, really can't. Honest I can't," she said, feeling Harry with her eyes closed because most times she dared not look at him.

"What's real?" Harry asked, moving out of reach. There were times when he did not appreciate being touched.

"You know what I mean," she said vaguely.

"I need shoes," said Harry, fingering his toes.

"Funny, I was just thinking that very thing today," she put in quickly.

"I need shirts," said Harry, rubbing a hand across his chest.

"Surprise! Surprise!" She reached under the bed and handed Harry a package. He stared dully through it.

"Hey, how far is it in miles to New York?" he finally asked, his voice trailing off as if he were already there.

"New York? You wondering about New York? Oh, it's far! Very far! Almost impossible to get to from here! You don't want to bother with New York."

She ran out and bought him six pairs of shoes.

She could not sleep for feasting and, after feasting, she was hungrier still and the more she dieted on Harry, the more the hollow bloomed inside. What was he doing to her? What wasn't he doing? She didn't know; she couldn't figure it out.

"What are you thinking about?" she asked him in bed late at night, as she could feel the tension curling like a spasm through his body. But he rarely answered. It was none of her business. He was thinking of himself.

"We've seen all the movies," he said to her one night as if she had been caught cheating.

"Oh, sweet Jesus, no!" she cried in a panic, rummaging through the newspaper listings. But he was right.

"We could stay home," she suggested.

"Sure," Harry mumbled.

"We could play cards. I used to be very good at cards. Hearts. I bet I could trounce you at hearts!"

Harry did not respond.

"Ha. Ha. I was only fooling. I bet you'd trounce me at hearts. You'd trounce me!" She bit her lip and frowned. Harry turned toward her and she quickly turned her frown into a smile, painfully cutting her lower lip by forgetting to remove her teeth from it.

"Sugar!" she cursed.

Harry did not hear her. He was working out decisions. Maybe it was good that they had run out of movies. Now there was no excuse to delay any further what he had so long delayed. Somewhere there had to be some answer to move him down some path to lead him to some future. RosalieMurchisonFrom*Macon?* was nice but she was beside the point. He treated her in the present as if she were already part of the past, as if she were a forgotten boiling kettle he'd come back to take off the stove while on his way to where he really wanted to go.

She felt the way she did as a child trying desperately to get the attention of a grownup, crying "Watch this! Watch this!" and throwing her skirt up over her head. Her skirt was over her head all the time now and it was clear that Harry was no longer watching. It was driving RosalieMurchisonFrom*Macon?* crazy. She loved him depressingly but her face was getting blowsy and she was looking overripe. Her posture had gone to hell along with her skin tone and soon her savings would be gone too and she knew Harry would be gone the next moment, gone to somebody else. There was a chorus line of factory women just waiting for him. And while she loved him to the point of losing herself, she retained that last remnant of shrunken ego that allowed the dream of stardom to go wasted but pulled up short when it came to her final survival.

One day she came home with a check for seven hundred dollars and an airline ticket to New York. It was the last of her savings. "Here," she said, handing him both check and ticket. "Hey, New York! That's a swell idea," said Harry, and he immediately began packing.

Harry flew away from RosalieMurchisonFrom*Macon?* on the first plane out of town. He had time to think during his drive to the airport, or rather, not so much to think as to allow his mind open to the whistling, stomping, dancing truths that the gesture of RosalieMurchisonFrom*Macon?* had inspired. How foolish his search, how needless the worries of the Harry Fund, of his parents, of his teachers. His direction was clear and had been clear from his earliest childhood, but the foggy sameness of his growing years had dimmed it. Insights ricocheted with heady celebration in the cabin of the plane.

Sweet RosalieMurchisonFrom*Macon?* had pointed his direction as if she were a laboratory experiment designed for that purpose. She had loved Harry. She had given him things. All of his life people had loved Harry, people had given him things. He reflected sadly on the formative years he was leaving behind and of the girl who, in a single act, had brought them into focus. He was sorry that, in all his excitement, he had forgotten to step in to say goodbye.

But he had no time to waste on sad thoughts. He let his mind settle pleasantly on what he would do from now on; what he would do for the rest of his life. He would do what he had always done. He would be loved.

PART TWO

HARRY,
THE
RAT
WITH
WOMEN

1.

Harry, the rat with women, entered his maturity looking more beautiful than ever; not beautiful in the normal way of men or women, nor even beautiful in the way he had previously been in his youth, but rather, beautiful as nature is beautiful. Looking at Harry was like looking at a sunset or a mountain range or the New York City skyline. He made people want to stand there reverently and watch; he made them want to salute. Sightseeing busses could have made a fortune driving around him.

He had filled his beauty as an animal fills its skin; all loose folds were taken up now, all details completed. Where in his growing days he had vibrated an excitement of change he now emitted calm: pure, uninvestigated, unrippled, uncaring calm. His beauty had settled in him like a well-poured foundation. It was not skin-deep but shone from beneath layers and layers suggesting that were the outer shell removed the glow at the core would be blinding.

He walked through the city and it purred and rolled over before him; the lights from windows only caught his face and left others in darkness; the sound of traffic softened to a bird's call and the air smelled of Indian summer. If Harry walked on one side of the street, as a sign of respect everyone else crossed over to the other.

He was loved with the sense of off-balanced urgency that is unique with the unrequited. The city ran up to him pleading, "Take me!" and, once taken, resented the taker for his lack of commitment. It shuffled miserably around him caught in a love trap, having to give and not being given in return; reflecting bitterly that Harry didn't really care, he was just taking advantage.

And Harry moved within it, never noticing. His touch left no finger-prints; almost anything could be proved by it. Those outside him belonged to a world apart, a universe he cared nothing for; dull, without shape, with-out definition. Their only possible excuse for being were as instruments for his comfort: their arms to carry presents, their mouths to offer praises, their bodies to satisfy his own body. Their eyes he used as mirrors.

"I can't decide what to do with my hair," he would say while staring into a lady's eyes. "I hate to trust it to anyone but myself. "

"Oh no, Harry, you mustn't."

"I'm the only one my hair really trusts."

"Your hair would trust *me*, Harry."

"Stop that, I just combed it! But if I cut it myself I can't do a really good job on the back —"

"Let me try, Harry. Your hair, your beautiful hair — "

"I told you to quit that. Do you know anyone who really knows how to press shirts? I mean people say they can press shirts but they come out either too soft or too stiff."

"Let me try, Harry. Please let me. I'm very good at pressing shirts."

"Sure, that's what you said about washing socks. Say, can't you get brighter lights in this room? I hate to see shadows all over my body."

He liked to present himself against various backgrounds; see how he looked against a blonde, how a brunette complemented the color of his eyelashes, how a redhead set off the tone of his skin. He covered the spectrum and back, resting easily wherever he desired and accepting only those parts of the worlds offered him that he might suddenly have a yen for. He had only to point, then he would taste and move on. His smiles shot and killed. He hunted with them carelessly and was well taken care of.

On his arrival in the city, he took a suite at the Waldorf. The management didn't charge; they thought he gave the building class.

"All I ask is to be taken care of," said Harry.

"All we ask is to die for you," answered the Waldorf. It was the answer he received everywhere.

He did not know how people knew about him. He accepted it as one of the interesting sidelights of New York; the way a big city makes welcome its strangers. His mail slot bulged with business: telephone messages beseeching private interviews, party invitations, letters from exclusive charities requesting his sponsorship, dinner invitations, theatre tickets compliments of Miss Blank I who bumped into him in the elevator, ballet tickets compliments of Miss Blank II who gave him her seat in the bar, a yachting invitation from Miss Blank III who followed him down Lexington Avenue in a taxi; love letters offering everything, asking nothing.

He became splendidly outfitted. "All we want is to die for you!" said the gentlemen from Sulka, Nica-Rattner, Battaglia, and Finchley. He added to his wardrobe carefully and if what he chose was not currently in mode his choosing it made it so. The closest thing to being Harry was to dress like Harry. Men, without knowing who he was, spotted him walking into a restaurant and walked out in imitation of his posture headed for a tasteful men's shop where they purchased Harry-style shirts, Harry-style ties, Harry-style cuff links. When Harry felt a drop of rain and slipped on his raincoat it was the raincoat signal up and down the avenue; within moments everyone had one on. When Harry felt a drop of rain but chose to ignore it — everyone got soaked.

"You don't want to go on living at the Waldorf," said beautiful, aging Mabel Thurston, often referred to as the Third Lady of the American Theatre.

"Don't I?" said Harry.

"It must be terrible for you to be taken care of by strangers."

"Oh, they're not such a bad bunch," said Harry.

"I can't allow it to continue! My twelve-room, nineteen-foot-ceilinged, view of the park duplex is at your service. Let me show you the *real* New York." Harry went along for the change.

2.

He was taken into a world of actors. Huge rooms full of smoke and show business, loud laughter from heads thrown back like weapons, booming with attention-seeking roars; backs massaged and arms squeezed, cheeks pinched and kisses thrown everywhere at random, even occasionally on the lips; an intimate family of names: "Jerry Baby! Marty Baby! Helen Baby! Alice Baby! Milton Baby! Edgar Baby! Marsha Baby! Dennis Baby! Doris Baby! Freddy Baby! Gladys Baby! Arthur Baby! Sir David Baby!" — the royal family of the theatre: the Babies.

And Mabel Baby and Harry Baby were their center. Harry glowed and Mabel entered Harry's glow and glowed alongside him. When she talked, it was Harry who was quoted: "It was either after my first *Antigone* or my second *Candida* that the critics started saying I had a great gusto for life.

Actually Doxie Wolheim was the first to say it and everyone picked it up from him. Doxie was always the first to say everything. Doxie was the first to say, 'Hollywood is where old age and talent go to retire.'"

Everyone chuckled at Harry.

"Doxie said everything first. When somebody at the Algonquin would say something clever, Doxie would always interrupt and tell him 'I said that yesterday.' And he had. Doxie said everything yesterday."

Everyone chuckled at Harry.

"But Doxie *was* the first to say it: 'Thurston,' he said to me, 'you have a great gusto for life.'

"'Doxie,' I replied, 'I am an actress, I have never heard of life. My great gusto is for sham.' Doxie was mortified that he hadn't said it first."

Everyone applauded Harry's story.

Actors have porous egos. Like the shark, who has no equipment to float so must swim all the time, the actor works always, whether employed or not, whether awake or not. He moves through a room of his own kind, each one seeing the other through a periscope that rises with intentions of looking out but always ends by turning back to inspect itself. "How'm I doing?" is the underground question rumbling through the room. "Beautiful, baby, beautiful," is the underground answer. Harry's presence drowned the answer. Party activity stopped when he entered the room. Glasses halted in mid-swoop, cigarettes paused and died. In any part of the room the word "Harry" was said often enough to lose all meaning.

"How are you feeling, Harry?"

"What did you do today, Harry?"

"Ha, ha! Stop it, you're killing me, Harry!"

"So I couldn't decide whether to get up or not."

"Is that the truth ? Wonderful, Harry!"

"So I got up. But then I went back to bed."

"Beautiful, Harry."

"Then I got up again."

"Too much, Harry! Too much!"

"Then I went back to sleep."

"Is that a story? Is that a beautiful story? That story breaks me up!

Charlie, Bernie, Eddie, Sid you just got to hear Harry's story!"

Harry was the center and there could be no other. The stars became his stagehands ("Have a drink, Harry"), forced always off to the side or into the background ("Harry, tell about the time you walked into the Oak Room and said to the maitre d' —"), eroded to the position of flunkies and orderlies ("You don't have a drink? Take my drink. You don't have a cigarette? Take my cigarette"), reduced to doing bits of business to get attention and, failing that, sinking completely into the anonymous claque surrounding Harry as if there lay some conciliatory distinction in being more splendidly anonymous, more compellingly anonymous, more anonymously anonymous than any of their co-stars.

But it had an effect: those actors who worked began giving gray performances on stage, smiling ingratiatingly at the audience as if there were seatfulls of Harrys out there waiting and not getting a drink; those without work signed quickly for a movie, any movie, to get them free of the city. They fled, and those that did not flee restrained themselves from attending parties that Harry might come and take from them. He was resented terribly but only in absentia; a casual meeting on the street and it would be "Harry Baby!" followed by an effusive demonstration to prove to all passersby that Harry was a close, close friend, a dear and good buddy.

Harry enjoyed his new world. He enjoyed the parties; he enjoyed the gifts received and he enjoyed the slumber-like moving from bed to bed. His pockets jingled with keys and if Mabel Thurston threw a tearful renunciation scene, he willingly offered to get out.

"Who said anything about getting out?" Mabel was forced to say. "Can't we ever have an intellectual discussion around here?"

He knew her apartment better than he knew her face; of which he was only certain by checking to see if it was the last one left at the end of an evening. Several times while on the street he'd call to a woman he thought was Mabel but who'd turn out to be someone else. It didn't matter. The time not spent in her west-side duplex could as well be spent with a model in a Gramercy Park triplex or another actress in an east-sixties brownstone.

"Harry, I don't want to be a prying woman. You know that."

"So?"

"But all I ask is when we have a date and you don't intend to show up — all I ask is: won't you please call and tell me?"

"Oh, sure, sure. Actually, that's a pretty good idea."

"I waited all night last night."

"Yes, that's a pretty good idea. I'll try to remember." But an hour later he'd forgotten with whom he had the conversation.

He was a narcotic and women had to have him; and like a narcotic, once the effect wore off there followed a slicing emptiness and a nervous need for more. Women staggered punch-drunk through the city, meeting and drinking excessively at luncheons, murmuring from table to table, "Harry's a rat, Harry's a rat, Harry's a rat."

In the usual course of events, Harry's casualness would probably not have earned him the reputation of being a rat with women; loving and leaving, while officially frowned on, seldom evokes a final, definitive judgment; many women enjoy being left only second best to being loved. Harry was not a rat for what he did but for what he didn't do. He left whomever he touched feeling untouched, whomever he dishonored feeling, regrettably, still honored. He left no aftertaste; no mark on the pillow. He was like summer thirst. He was like Chinese food. Once he was gone, nothing had been there.

He was never the flirt. A flirt is conscious of the game; Harry's game involved only himself. For that reason there was no defense against him.

As in myths or fairy tales, knight errants (in this case, women) marched on horseback toward him bellowing the challenge "Joust if you dare, Sir Harry!" Titillated with rumors of his invincibility, hosts of heavily armored ladies rose tall from behind their breasts, cornered him in his love nest and threw down their gauntlets — followed shortly by their armor, their defiance and their souls. And the more stories spread about his irresistibility, the more challenges received. Love in Harry's time was not love at all; it was imperialism.

Once, far back in history, Love, like Fire, began as a utility. Its job was to fill the hours between the end of work and the beginning of sleep and, like other tools, it was used only when it was the right instrument for the job. No one talked about it; no one sang about it; no one wrote poems about it. Songs and poems were saved for the primary tools such as Fire.

But the time given over to Love declined. It was an unaggressive tool; of no use in war or conquest. It petered out and disappeared; and the only warmth left to man was Fire. And out of Fire a new Love was born, no longer a pacifist but a conqueror. It spread like blight, ravaging lives and creating a myth of its name. With the myth it tried to conquer the world.

Love, the imperialist, sent forth its missionaries into virgin territory. As soon as Love's myth was planted and a single speculative gate began to rise Love, rammed the gate, demanded tribute and ran up its black flag: Possession.

Love's myth spread and with it the warning of its heavy bounty. Defenses were mounted against it. Instruction was given in identifying the myth. Self-examination was encouraged for nullifying the myth. Numbness was recommended for making the myth less dangerous. Love was prepared for, conquered and disemboweled. From that time, every act between two people was further celebration of its demise.

Love died as an act leaving its word behind as a corpse. The dead word was nailed to the shields of lovers and carried bravely into battle.

Lovers fought without knowing who it was they fought; they bled and never learned why. They felt deeply their imitated emotions. Becoming battle-weary and sensing that victory did not exist, they deserted the field. They hid at home and constructed shells for themselves. But the shells were on the inside. They became walking, talking, living, breathing fortresses. One example was Georgette Wallender.

3.

She was small but looked large; she was pretty but looked formidable; she was softly built but looked indestructible. She had cool eyes; the eyes of an appraiser, steady as two black buttons and operating like reverse mirrors: they could see out; no one could see in. Her interior was a well-stocked dungeon of reserve against a hostile world; her exterior was a symbol of the hardness in that very world she saw as hostile.

In the company of other women she could act fairly open if not trusting, for despite the private claims of each they were all on record as being in it together; NATO allies to the end. With men her openness clouded; an affair working warmly would suddenly chill. No one knew why. Love would tentatively begin and then, at a point just short of fruition, stop cold, not receding but vanishing quickly; embarrassed for having been where it wasn't wanted. From inside her wall she sent out signals of peace to the world: her womanliness, her composure, her silent promise that the game was more than worth the candle. Men picked up the signals like dropped handkerchiefs. The circle would form again: first hard, then soft, then gone. She would withdraw her hand, and softly say, "It's time, my dear, we had a serious conversation," and immediately afterward add to her bulging portfolio one more new friend; someone to lunch with once a month and be advised on the condition of the market.

Georgette met Harry at a party to which she had gone in order to break off with her current lover, a gentleman over whom she was becoming fond. She preferred to make her farewells at parties; in private they could become embarrassing. In addition, she deemed it only fair to the man to part with him in a crowd and afford him a chance of finding another girl to take home. She was expert at these occasions and performed less like a participant than a hostess; doing her utmost to make her guest feel as comfortable as possible in his new, unfamiliar surroundings. Soothingly, they had oozed from lovers to sweethearts to buddies. Their faces were aglow with mutual affection; Georgette's because she never felt so close to a man as when she broke off with him and the young man's because he was convinced that he had somehow won a great victory by surrendering everything. Their hands slid lingeringly apart as they went their private ways: he to the bar to celebrate his mature handling of a difficult situation and Georgette to another room where her eyes landed and fixed forever on Harry.

"My name is Georgette Wallender," she said.

"I'm Harry," Harry said.

"I want you to know you can never hurt me," she said. She took his hand and wouldn't let go.

Georgette had known of Harry for some time before they met — not by name but by feeling. He had been the background music to her life, playing counter to her own theme: the rising crescendo heard in all the romantic novels of her childhood, in all the bad films and radio plays. Her shell opened and took him in. Then, still impregnable, it closed around him.

"I love. I know I love," she said to the Harry buried inside her. The Harry outside barely responded.

"Love is a vast prairie — " she frowned. "No, rather it's a flower on that prairie — a desert flower, fragile and full at the same time. Alone. Exquisitely alone and yet rooted deeply in the nestling soil. No, it isn't." She frowned again and tried to get more deeply into herself. "Love is a straight line going off into infinity; a series of vari-angled planes. No, that's wrong. Love is architecture — no, it's richer than that. Love is — is candy. Sweet and deep. And sticky. Like toffee. No, that's shallow. Love is — wait a minute — I had it a second ago —"

"I think love is smooth and creamy," said Harry, thinking of himself.

"I had it a second ago — What the devil did I mean to say?" Georgette asked the Harry inside her.

"I think love is like white bread," said the outside Harry, beginning to feel hungry.

But Georgette not only loved; she was a commentator on love. She thrilled to the sound of her own descriptions: "I sit in judgment of my love for you. When we wake up in the morning the first thing I think of is, 'do I still love you?' Immediately there's this quickening in my chest. Right here," she indicated her heart, "and I know the answer is, 'yes'. But then I ask myself *how* much do I love you? How much do I really love you on a scale of one to ten? And the answer is ten!

"When I'm at the office I become frightened once I begin thinking of the job. Does it mean I've stopped loving you? I quickly hold myself here," she indicated her heart, "and ask myself if I love you. And all day at the office you score ten!

"At night when we're together I often think that I will die if I look into your eyes. What if I look into them and find that I really don't love you? I struggle to avoid your eyes but I know sooner or later I must judge. So I do look into your eyes. And I feel this quickening — you know, right here — and once more you score a ten!" She looked at Harry proudly as if he had just won an award, "You and your tens."

They held hands and Georgette stared deeply at the space above Harry's eye. "Ours is a classic love."

Love became more real when she talked about it; and to go back and talk about it some more made it more real than real; an improvement on the original. She turned it into living theatre at the luncheon table. Her now narrowing circle of women friends listened heavily; their pill-box hats rising to each climax like surfboards on a wave, their breathing so deep that in a room full of cigarette smoke their comer stood out with the clarity of an etching.

"Be careful," they warned. Georgette beamed. "You don't know what love is," she said carelessly. It was an accurate appraisal.

4.

Her friends, like herself, were highly successful business women — diverse in interests but equal in rank: ambitious, socially conscious and quietly powerful. Their power had begun small but flourished as rumor of its potency was spread, first by themselves and later by others. The rumor was eventually accepted as the truth and so became true; their influence was felt everywhere.

Society in Harry's time operated on a descending spiral of oligarchies. The limits of each oligarchy were defined by its position on the spiral. At the top formed a hierarchy of business, politics and the military; a mixed bag of interchanging personnel who laid down the broad rules from which all laws were derived. Under this primary control group all secondary oligarchies twirled. Directly below was the political oligarchy; split neatly into a responsible left and a responsible right — free to range widely in all directions as long as they stopped short at the prescribed boundaries.

Spiraling under the political oligarchy was the ethical oligarchy whose rules were jointly established by a free exchange (within the limits of their level) of business and religious groups. From there the spiral twisted into an intricately tightening whirl. Georgette's friends operated on one of its lower middle levels; a substratum whose freedom to debate was considered complete though all the positions taken clung well within their narrow level. They operated their oligarchy coldly and efficiently. Their single interest lay in the area they liked to describe as "The battle of the sexes." They fought it well and for good reason. It was the one area left where it was safe to do battle.

They knew each other (in order of importance) by income, by rank, by name and by appearance — a closely meshed circle of accomplishment meeting often at lunch, cocktails and dinner, pulling strings, managing lives and exchanging inside stories; the married members escorted by their robust, cologne-smelling husbands, the single ones adorned with the currently voguish ballad singer, actor, designer, photographer or playwrights. She: bold as brass, he: soft as dawn.

The group leader (and so recognized) was the syndicated gossip columnist and television panelist Belle Mankis, adored by her friends who called her "Our darling Belle," unadored by her enemies who called her "Preying Mankis."

Whomever Belle saw fit to use as an intimate became part of the group.

Naomi Peel, famed psychoanalyst, physical therapist and television panelist; author of the daily column of frank advice, "God and Your Heart"; a dedicated foe of homosexuality and intermarriage; also known as "the psychiatrist to the stars."

India Anderbull, famed novelist and television panelist; winner of the National Book Award for *The Weaklings*, a novel of the husband in America; creator of the Emmy-Award family television series "The Weaklings," a more humorous treatment of the same subject.

Arlene Moon, famed publicist and television panelist; best known for her unpublicized religious works; a dedicated foe of smut.

Viola Strife, famed lawyer and television panelist; best known for her lucrative settlements in divorce litigation; a passionate advocate of legally strengthening the marital vows.

And Georgette, who, aside from her duties as a television panelist, edited *Outré*, the women's fashion magazine.

To all of them and to Georgette too until she met Harry, men were a social convenience; things to date when they went out with the girls at night. Marriage was condoned as either an early mistake, a career necessity or a financial arrangement. Women, they had long ago discovered, got along best with other women. As a group they lived for themselves as Harry lived for himself and because of this they were freer of his allure than most women; not free enough to dismiss him, but free enough to be able not to love him — though he did confuse them terribly. Georgette's infatuation had blown a hole in their ranks. In Harry's presence they felt defensive (a new feeling around men) and out of control (a new feeling around anybody).

Power was the central force of their lives. It ushered them into night clubs, theatres, fashionable restaurants. It paid their bills, it bought their tickets, it sent them free books. They were courted by the needy and the publicity seekers and, after years of doling out harsh experience, were given a group name: The Blue Belles.

They were a male morality watchdog society: giving speeches, writing papers, arguing on television and, as members of a private underground, doing more — much more. They acted as spotters of the rich and eligible: men of indiscriminate age with sufficient funds and reputation to benefit themselves or their colleagues. Once the mark was spotted an invisible circle was drawn around him. Only one of their own was permitted inside to drink, to dine, to make love, to marry. Outsiders were frightened off. The total power of the middle level was directed at them: a call to the phone where an anonymous voice lay down the penalties of trespass — to be gossip columned, public relationed, and legal actioned to death. Outsiders quickly learned the boundary lines of fun and withdrew.

They operated as the game wardens of society. Those women who would not scare were made examples of. The few men who challenged the circle were laid open to public attack and private harassment; called away from their tables at restaurants to hear the whispered telephone message, "Get rid of the bitch. Get rid of the bitch." Or, if subtlety were the evening's plan, no message at all — only heavy breathing.

It was a sorority game and the Blue Belles brought to it the spirit of the natural game player. Whether this game or any other, they relished the excitement of tit-for-tatmanship. Games were a way of life, a private language, a means of communication. Talk was cheap and unrewarding; games were the true religion. They played them with rising ecstasy and found joy in their celebration.

They played "Botticelli," "Twenty Questions," "Ghosts," "Geography," "Fact or Fiction," "Silent Movies," "Coffee Pot," "Capistrano," "Minestrone," "Arthur's Mother," "Bride and Groom," "Self-Destruction," and many others — around the clock till the night was gone and early morning was over and no one could think of what to do next except go home.

Belle Mankis hated that moment.

"There must be at least one more game," she insistently said as the guests shuffled into their coats and kissed goodbye. She called out names. "Did we play 'Augmenting'?"

"Yes, we played 'Augmenting,'" one of her guests said tiredly.

"Did we play 'Arraignment'?"

But they had played that too; and every other game as well.

Her friends started to leave. Belle followed them despondently. "Wait!" she cried with inspiration.

"We didn't play 'Doctor'!"

"'Doctor's' a *children's* game," growled India Anderbull. But Belle made them play it.

"How do you know it isn't fun if you don't try?"

As it turned out it was fun; more fun than almost anything. They added it to the top of the list.

Harry was as much an irritant in games as he was in everything else. Winning or losing seemed beside the point to him and he let the tension of the contest flag as he thought over his position carefully, often distracted by other thoughts and really not caring in the slightest, till the men disbanded into small drinking circles and the women, if they could, would have screamed. But they couldn't with Harry. He watered their malice and made the act worse by being unaware of it.

One night they played "Super-Truth," a game in which each player had to reveal a single unpleasant characteristic that he found in all the other players. Harry's turn came but he could think of nothing unpleasant to say about anyone.

"Even me?" teased Belle Mankis.

"I suppose I never paid attention," said Harry.

"There must be some unpleasant characteristic in at least one of us," said Viola Strife.

All the Blue Belles laughed.

"I suppose I never bothered to notice," said Harry.

"Georgette!" cried Belle. "You certainly must have noticed Georgette."

Everyone applauded. Georgette smiled and pretended to blush.

More applause and shrieks of fun.

"Oh, sure," said Harry.

"Give us an unpleasant characteristic," said Belle.

And the Blue Belles leaned forward.

Georgette smiled to herself, knowing that poor, bewildered, hopelessly in love Harry could have no answer.

"For one thing," began Harry, "she's always around." The sound of raising eyebrows filled the room. Georgette's expression did not change but over it there suddenly appeared a series of fine lines.

5.

Here was her first hint that Harry was not her slave. She had opened herself to this man, given him love, trusted and become dependent on him, bought him gifts, given him a place to live and now: he was slipping away.

If she confronted Harry with the truth she was sure he'd deny it, poor dear. He would have thrown himself at her feet and protested that his comment was merely a joke, a silly, misplaced party remark; but Georgette knew that, though neither of them wanted to admit it, the sign was there. So it was senseless to reveal her insight to him. She was the stronger of the two and if a solution were to be found she would have to be the one who found it. One thing was clear from the beginning; she would not let him go.

Having decided all this in a matter of moments, Georgette felt refreshed. Her depression lifted as do all depressions once a decision is arrived at. Their future was in her small, capable hands and with that knowledge she could afford to be patient. She would observe Harry and find a way of banishing his doubts.

The new lines on her face softened but did not disappear. During the next weeks she watched him unsparingly. Whenever Harry looked up from his private interests he saw her damp, soft eyes, blind with understanding.

She was all over him; gentle, sweet, reassuring — as if they were no longer lovers. She asked Harry questions; she urged him to talk about himself, knowing it was a way of keeping him interested; she tried to draw him out. But somehow the questions she asked were unending, with parts one, two, three; subtopics A, B, C, and D; interspersed with pithy observations on life and love that might have told Harry, had he not been winding his watch, more about their own situation than she intended. One part of her heard but could not halt that cool, calm wisdom-dropping voice taking off on its endless display:

"When I was a child I always stayed in the house. I always believed that if I went outside I would get hit. My parents encouraged me to go outside. My teachers encouraged me to go outside. Aunts and uncles whom I loved encouraged me to go outside. So I did. And I got hit. Experience doesn't teach; it merely confirms.

"So, I withdrew from the outside world and decided never to be vulnerable again. But I learned that if one hides oneself from hurt one hides oneself from love. Harry, dear, we are really very much alike, you and I. We are practically the same person. Will you please stop winding your watch?"

Georgette understood in detail the effect her insights would have upon Harry; they would cause guilt and his guilt would cause him to resent her and his resentment would force him to strike out in boyish rebellion. So she was not surprised to find that he had begun dating other women. When Belle Mankis reported the news Georgette insisted that it was not yet time to discipline him; he would be allowed his fling and yet be made aware that, rebellious or not, his Georgette was always there.

And she was. Whenever Harry took a new love to dine, there, alone at the table across the room, sat Georgette, a soft light playing on her wide-brimmed hat, her dark glasses and veil never quite concealing the understanding smile charging his way. For the first six weeks he thought it a coincidence.

Late at night with Harry ensconced in his new apartment, Georgette, for whom no phone number was unlisted, would wake him, laugh warmly into the receiver and say, "Harry, you poor dear, you're really having quite a time for yourself. I just want you to know that I think it's all wonderful."

Occasionally, when Harry wasn't home, she'd be almost through with her message before realizing she had gotten the answering service.

Harry's new girl became upset. "That woman won't leave us alone! Not that I want to complain, Harry."

Her name was Faith Maynard, a gentle-faced girl with large hands who worked as an interior decorator. Harry was first attracted to her when she convinced him that she could reproduce *him* in the form of an apartment. But while her execution was brilliant, her conception was shallow. From the beginning Harry felt the apartment a disappointment. He didn't know much about interior design but he knew whether it was *him* or not. The chairs were *him*, the rugs were *him*, but the curtains, the tables, the wall decorations and the German icons were definitely nobody's and the canopied bed with its welter of silk hangings could never be *him*, it was obviously *her*. It was just such unobtrusive insincerity that annoyed Harry the most. He moved in with her, expecting to move out immediately.

"What woman won't leave us alone?" Harry said, listening to the sound of his own voice. He kept forgetting that he must have Faith add a tape recorder to the apartment.

"*You* know who I mean! The woman who keeps calling!"

"Oh, Georgette!" laughed Harry. "You mean Georgette. I didn't know you knew her."

"I don't."

"Then why do you mind her calling me? She's only a friend. She just thinks I need looking after."

"She's trying to get you back," brooded Faith.

"Do you really think so?" mused Harry. His respect for Georgette catapulted.

Now that he took the time to think of it, perhaps Faith was right: the meetings in restaurants, the phone calls, the flood of endearing mementos; he had never been besieged like this. No other woman had the nerve. They had always let go of him easily, hoping he'd remember and return, fearing that if they threw the fit they wanted to, they would lose him forever. And so they turned into what Harry had always seen them as; inanimate objects who had somehow learned the trick of animation. They walked, they talked, they offered love; and they accepted rejection with that heartwarming, defenseless little smile guaranteed to break every heart except the heart aimed at.

How thin and characterless Georgette made them seem. While admittedly a few had followed him down the street, pleading, and others had called him late at night, these were obvious acts of hysteria — not a planned campaign, not a tenacious holding action like Georgette's. A curtain had lifted and Harry now saw that she dogged his every step from the moment he left her; and yet she did not cry — she did not seem on the defensive. It was as if walking backward were the most natural and agreeable of acts. "How magnificent," he thought. In a vague way Harry was becoming interested.

He had never known suspense in his dealings with women; there had never been any question about the outcome. But this strange woman refused to vanish; it shifted the balance. Harry felt a new anticipation, a new fondness for her. He viewed her with growing sympathy as the underdog in a losing contest, hopeful that despite the great odds against her she might surprise him and win. He did not see himself as her opponent but as her claque. The next time she called and woke him he wished her luck, cheered her on and moved back in with her.

Georgette felt like a giantess! Here he was, docilely in her arms again; Georgette's triumph! She knew now that love had been a test not to weaken but to strengthen her. Harry, who was known as a rat with women, had crumbled. She had not begged, she had not demeaned; she had mastered. It would all be much easier now. She had proved to him who was the stable and the strong one; it would no longer be a struggle. He would bend to her will, listen and learn from her.

Their separation allowed her to see him more clearly now: he was so much the boy; a spoiled, bewildered, self-indulgent, beautiful boy. She would take this boy and train him to be a man. Only then would she marry him. Her days of blind love were over; Harry had better rise to her or she might someday leave him. She dreaded the thought. What would Harry do if she left him? He had left her and it had made her strong. She feared it would be just the opposite with Harry. He would collapse — might even kill himself. She grew angry; she was a busy woman and wasn't at all sure she had time for all this responsibility. She thought of him as he cheerfully unpacked in the next room, noisily pulling out drawers, clumsily banging into things. She smiled thinly at the immensity of the job that lay ahead; then she went inside to teach him how to put away his socks.

6.

"You know the trouble with you, Harry?"

Harry looked up encouragingly. It was their second week back together, and now that Georgette was no longer talking about her own state of mind but his, he found her much more fun.

"You're withdrawn. You don't communicate."

"What do you know!" said Harry.

"It's one of the big problems in society today — in the world, as a matter of fact — the breakdown in communication."

"I'd rather have a good time," said Harry.

"You poor dear, don't you see that without communicating you can't have a good time?"

"Oh, I enjoy myself," said Harry.

"False enjoyment is not happiness, Harry. God put us on this earth to communicate; else why did he give us language?"

"I use language. Listen, sometimes I never stop talking."

"We don't use language, any more; we *misuse* it. Language is no longer a means of communication but a means of avoiding communication."

"You can't make the world over," said Harry. Georgette placed his head between her hands and forced herself to stare into his eyes; they were miles away.

"Communication isn't easy, Harry dear. Believe me, I know that. But all we have left is to try. We communicate a little today. We communicate a little more tomorrow. And who knows, but someday soon — *total* communication."

She let her hands leave his face. His eyes had outdistanced her.

"But you — what do you do, Harry?"

His eyes came back. "Tell me!"

"You go around in your own private world. Never communicating. Never making contact.

That's why you can't be happy. You're afraid to leave your shell. Insecure and afraid!"

Harry began to look interested. Georgette ran on, sensing a breakthrough.

"Don't you see, my dearest? Once you're able to make contact, a permanent contact with somebody, some special person, you will be happy. You'll have to be. Because you'll be fulfilled."

She let her fingers run through his hair.

"You poor dear, not a word I said has penetrated, has it?"

"Don't do that; I just combed it," said Harry.

He now had something new to think about. Georgette was sketching in a different world. He vaguely remembered some of her ideas; they had been covered in school, but they hadn't really registered. A fresh hunger awakened in Harry; a new part of himself was lying there — waiting to be explored. He looked forward to Georgette's lectures.

"Talk to me."

"What am I going to do with you, Harry?"

"Talk to me. Tell me about the breakdown in communication."

"I've told you."

"Tell me about my not making contact."

"I've told you. Dozens of times."

"Tell me again. I forgot."

"Harry, you don't listen."

"Sure, I do. I listen to *you*. Tell me about the breakdown in communication." He rested at her feet, looked innocently up and waited

The lines in Georgette's face deepened. Working with Harry was like building with papier-mâché; each time she'd seem to have a construction going it would depart into formlessness. If he were trying to control her she would have known how to handle it; she still had no doubt who was the stronger in a contest of wills. But Harry gave her no chance to demonstrate; he refused to be the opposition. He abdicated amiably, bending to her iron will though she had hardly begun to exercise it. Part of her pride in regaining him lay in the confirmation of the strength she had always supposed was hidden within her: an underground soldier lying in wait for the command. But once that strength was unleashed it needed action; it needed further proof of its invincibility. And instead, what did the enemy give her? A form of surrender so good-natured, so all-embracing that it made her own aggression seem trivial almost passive. Like any other peacetime militarist, her inner soldier grumbled and grew confused. There are those old soldiers who much prefer dying to fading away.

The balance had tipped in his favor again; yet Georgette could not remember the moment of change. Her lectures had lost their inspirational outer layer and had assumed a personal whine. She knew Harry was not seeing other women; there wasn't time. Nevertheless she called Belle Mankis and asked her to check around. She knew he was becoming bored again.

"Harry, please listen to me. Really it's getting serious, this breakdown in communication of yours. Honestly, you've got to learn to make contact. You'll never be happy until you do. I'm saying this because I want to help you. I wish I had somebody to tell me the things I'm telling you. Please listen to me, Harry."

7.

One day India Anderbull reported spotting Harry having cocktails at her sports club with a well-known female tennis star. The Blue Belles called a meeting. Georgette sat through it not hearing a word, just shaking her head.

"Harry's a rat," Belle Mankis began.

There followed a chorus of grumbled ayes.

"We let him off the hook once — for Georgette's sake," said India Anderbull, circling her small friend with a heavy arm. "I was against it! You all remember how I was against it!"

"There's no point in reworking the past!" counseled Viola Strife.

"You let one of those sons of bitches off the hook and they all get ideas," said Naomi Peel.

"We've been too easy," said Arlene Moon.

"Harry's had it," said Belle Mankis.

Five thumbs pointed down.

"We'll make an example of him."

Then they ordered cocktails and talked about other things. The decision had been made and was irrevocable.

"Let me talk to him once more," Georgette pleaded, "I'll explain every-thing — "

Georgette was clearly in a state of shock. They sent her to a rest home.

Harry's telephone began to ring late at night.

"Hello."

"You son of a bitch. You son of a bitch. You son of a bitch!"

"Oh, hi Naomi!"

"Don't 'Hi Naomi' me, Harry! You're a dirty rat! Besides, I'm not Naomi."

"Hey, I'm glad you called. Georgette has gone away somewhere and she forgot to pay this month's rent and I don't know where in the world I'm going to get it."

There was a long sullen pause at the other end.

"How much do you need?" the voice said.

They were no more effective with Harry's women. Of what concern was a career when Harry could be there to comfort them? "Gee, I'm sorry you've been fired," he told one beautiful lady after another; but only when their cash reserves dwindled did they discover that they had suffered two losses, not one.

8.

"You're dead in this town," the 4 A.M. phone call told him. "Pack up and get out!"

"Hi, Belle. Say, how come we never run into each other any more?" greeted Harry.

9.

The situation had become impossible for the Blue Belles. Harry was more than just a goad to one of their members; he was a threat to the existence of the organization. If he outlasted their onslaught their reputation would be disastrously weakened. It was revolutionaries such as Harry who made it bad for entrenched systems everywhere. Were he to survive much longer who knew what rabbit-spined millionaire would take courage from his example and defy their authority? The issue had become bigger than Harry. It had turned into a test case.

Extremes were required. They decided to send for Eugenie Vasch. They wired her care of Claridge's, London. The return cable arrived the next morning: "Currently engaged full-time wrecking member of Parliament. Have Thursdays free. Wire if sufficient."

The Blue Belles cabled back that it would have to be.

10.

Except for some hard lines around the jaw, Eugenie Vasch was every bit as beautiful as Harry. She was, until a series of unfortunate scandals, regularly on the list of best-dressed women of the world, and this without her own fortune. Eugenie squandered money the moment it came within reach. Having it depressed her, and having men with it depressed her even more. She spent the money, broke the man and went off to adventure elsewhere. Men were as helpless with her as women with Harry. But Harry could also be loved by men; the Blue Belles aside, other women hated Eugenie. Her very presence was an attack on their sexuality; making them feel not like women at all, but some interim sex. She was the complete female and yet success at it kept eluding her. She kept winding up in illegalities that damned her reputation and only allowed her to exist in her lovers' private lives. Publicly they were forced to ignore her. She despised men — not as cowards or weaklings or helpless boys — but as men. She had purified the Blue Belles' philosophy into an art. It was this art that she practiced in order to make a living: she was a freelance castrater.

In her past and for no profit, she had reduced to impotence movie stars, diplomats, heads of state, heads of magazine chains, industrialists, sportsmen, philanthropists, pacifists, literary lights —men who afterward bitterly cursed her betrayal while wistfully cherishing the flaccid remains of their lost love.

But that had been for fun; now she was a business woman. Wives on the hunt for revenge against husbands who cheated them sexually or spiritually summoned Eugenie from across the world to cancel permanently their mates' masculinity; to cripple them so that no woman would ever again desire to use them except their wives. It was no trick to compel her victims to become infatuated; the trick was to entrap them before they could let go, and even more, to enlist them as willing conspirators to their own debasement.

Her past romances met for drinks and exchanged the same stories:

"I don't know exactly what it was but it seemed clear from the beginning that she was better than I was."

"Yes, exactly."

"And yet she didn't seem to recognize it. Not only was I treated as an equal; but in many ways as a superior."

"Of course. Of course."

"I became better than myself: brighter, wittier, more lucid. I began to feel released. I began to feel that I knew so much more than I ever dared dream — . She'd look up at me with those enormous, trusting violet eyes —"

"Yellow: they were yellow. Cat's eyes."

"Violet. Definitely violet."

"Yellow."

"Violet."

"Yellow."

"Definitely violet!"

"Indeed? Well, she was certainly all things to all men, wouldn't you say?"

"Well put. Extremely well put. At any rate, those eyes — a moment's stare made me swell like a balloon; an encouraging comment made me feel like a king!"

"Yes, but didn't you feel like a hoax all the while?"

"Exactly. As I grew larger in her eyes I felt that she was sure to find me out one of these days; that I would do or say the wrong thing and she'd suddenly see me for what I really was."

"Indeed."

"A very little man."

"Oh, really, not so little as all that."

"I meant in her eyes."

"Oh, of course."

"I had heard about her; I knew what she was supposed to be."

"But that didn't hold you back."

"I accepted the rumors. I could see their grounds for validity; but a dubious validity; a hostile validity; a validity born out of the incapability of others to handle her."

"And you could handle her."

"Not unless she wanted me to handle her. And that was the wonderful part of it : the sense that elevated me to the class of giants! I saw in her eyes that, ridiculous as it may have seemed, *I* was the one she had chosen to tame her."

"Indeed."

"She would be different with me. Because *I* was different."

"Indeed."

"So I fell in love. The problem with middle-aged love is that its seriousness rises in proportion to its lack of reality. If you think a woman has fallen in love with an inflated image of you, you'd much rather break your neck than not live up to it."

"So you *did* live up to it?"

"One does what one can. After several months I was like an exhausted channel swimmer. And yet she never seemed to notice. Each time I felt that I was about to sink back to my real level, her hand went out and pulled me up beside her. Well, after years of marriage, one is not used to this degree of support from a woman."

"There must have been a reason."

"Yes. And I concluded that the reason was that, whether I knew it or not, I *was* better; I was different; I was what I never dared dream I was: a truly romantic figure."

"A truly romantic figure."

"And that is when she began to change."

"Ah, yes."

"The remarks began."

"How well I remember. The remarks."

"Nothing one could put his finger on."

"Oh, no."

"But deflating nonetheless; indicating something definitely wrong. And it wasn't just the remarks. Her eyes, those eyes that always before had stared at me and only me, now began to wander. I couldn't seem to catch them. They'd be on me and suddenly they'd swing away. And stay away."

"You mentioned it to her, of course."

"Ours was an affair of great honesty. We told each other everything. I could no more keep the truth from her than confide in my wife."

"And she denied everything."

"As a matter of fact she became rather ironic. She apologized for the deficiency of her *eyes*. She requested that I list for her all those remarks of which I did not approve."

"And you couldn't remember any."

"Damn it, it's impossible to document a *feeling*. I wanted to both prove and disprove my contentions. I felt like an absolute ass!"

"Which she indicated."

"No, she was sympathetic. She looked at me with great patience in her eyes. It seemed to negate everything I was saying. She denied everything. She couldn't understand why I was acting so silly. My behavior was ridiculous and not at all like me. Or perhaps she was mistaken; perhaps it *was* exactly like me."

"Then, naturally, *you* denied everything."

"Of course. I said there'd been great strain at the department. Several governments in danger of toppling. I wasn't myself. Forgive me."

"You're mumbling. What was that last?"

"Forgive me."

"Ah, yes, forgive me."

"From then on we never seemed to meet at the same level. I kept insisting that something must be wrong. She kept denying it. And then I noticed she had stopped wearing my presents."

"Somebody else's?"

"Possibly yours."

"Mm. Quite possible."

"And yet I could never get anything out of her. I was out of my mind with jealousy. I said to her if you want to end it let's end it! Just don't leave me hanging like this in mid-air!"

"And her reply?"

"She turned angrily away and said she didn't know what I was talking about but if I insisted on acting so petulantly — "

"Ah, yes — petulantly."

"— then she was not going to see me that evening; in any event she had made other plans. I told her that if she had made other plans, she had made them before I acted 'petulant' and therefore I was correct in assuming that there was something wrong between us. She turned on me and I had never seen her stare at me so coldly. And I will never forget the words she spoke to me."

"I believe I can guess them."

"She looked at me as if I had a growth on my nose and said plainly and strongly, as if to a teen-age street molester — 'What's—bothering—you?'"

"Ah, yes, 'What's—bothering—you?'"

"I needn't tell you how brutal it was from that point on. She was busy; she was out; she couldn't be reached on the telephone; she didn't answer my wires. When I finally saw her, she acted as if it were all in my mind, as if nothing had happened."

"She was warm again?"

"It was like old times. How could I have been so mistaken? My hopes were buoyed. I rejoiced.

Talked madly. Made plans."

"Then suddenly she had to get home early?"

"You know it. There it all was. Every reborn joy of the evening lying gutted all over the dinner table. I said — "

"'But I have theatre tickets.'"

"Yes, that's what I said and she said — "

"'It was a lovely evening, don't spoil it.'"

"Exactly. And I asked, 'When will I see you again?' I no longer dared let her out of my sight without making a new and definite date. Otherwise, I'd never be able to catch her."

"And she said, 'Call me tomorrow. I'll be in all morning.'"

"And she was gone."

"And you called all morning."

"And I never got an answer."

"I weep for both of us."

11.

On the Thursday that Eugenie Vasch flew in from London to take care of some quick business, Harry lay around wondering what to do with himself. Georgette had quickened his desire for the exotic. He found his new women dull. When he spoke to them about philosophies of life they looked at him blankly or talked about motherhood. When he suggested that modern society was beset by a breakdown in communication they mumbled something about monopoly and Bell Telephone. Georgette might have been a bore but there was a facet of her to which he'd responded: her concern with issues that did not exist for Harry. All that fuss she made about making contact as if there were a point in doing something just for the sake of it — like taking English in school when it was clear that one would never use it. Make contact — with whom? Learn to communicate — with whom? People had always given him their attention. If he was less interesting than they, why weren't they devoting that time to themselves? Was it "communication" for Harry to pay attention to others while, in exchange, they paid attention to him? It sounded like a bad bargain. He sensed that most people's lives were made up of inventing excuses for not getting what they wanted. Perhaps that was what this whole business of contact and communication was. The thinkers of the world were the losers.

Nevertheless he was dissatisfied. He had no desire to be alone and less desire to be with others. What's more, he missed Georgette. He wished she'd return with some new lectures. Perhaps that was what she was up to, he thought happily. She was in a school — taking courses — learning lectures to bring back to Harry! The idea cheered him considerably. He began to dress, having decided to put in an appearance at a party that in his previous mood he had intended to skip. The Blue Belles would be there, and if he were not seen enjoying himself, they might forget to call. Their nightly messages had become his one constant pleasure.

The moment Harry entered the big room Belle Mankis, Naomi Peel, Viola Strife, Arlene Moon and India Anderbull closed in around him. "Harry, there's someone in the next room we know you'll want to meet!"

Four days later Harry and Eugenie Vasch were married.

12.

Eugenie was moved by Harry as she had never been moved by any man: slightly. It was a peculiar feeling, in its own way, even pleasurable. He intrigued her — not for his own special qualities but for the changes within her these qualities evoked. Her world was as self-absorbed as Harry's; how long, she wondered, would these new feelings last? A week? A month? Then would she hate him? She was curious to find out. Harry remained as shadowy in her eyes as her other men, but theirs were imperfect shadows; Harry's was perfect. His beauty, while apparent, did not strike her with awe; she was equally beautiful — and this, she excused, was probably the reason for her interest. He was her equal.

"People don't seem to make contact any more," said Harry, as a way of beginning their first conversation.

"I think that's a stupid subject. But I think everything is a stupid subject," answered Eugenie.

Harry suddenly noticed her. "Do you really? So do I. As a matter of fact I always have."

"People are so universally uninteresting! I usually don't say that when I meet a man because he generally thinks I'm referring to him."

"Why in the world would he think that" wondered Harry.

"Most everything is cheap, rotten, corrupt, and disgusting," said Eugenie.

"Well, you're certainly entitled to your point of view, but I find people are pretty much the same the world over."

"I wish I could show you Madrid," said Eugenie, making a languid hand motion as if to describe it.

"Is it beautiful?"

"It's ugly," said Eugenie, "but it's an ancient, honest ugliness. The closest one comes to beauty in this world is uncorrupted ugliness."

"I've never really noticed," said Harry. "I only notice what I want to. That way everything is beautiful."

"Nothing is beautiful," said Eugenie.

"I am."

"So am I," said Eugenie. "But what are we underneath?"

"I'm beautiful underneath," said Harry.

"No one is," said Eugenie.

"I'm beautiful all the way down."

"We are both beautiful," said Eugenie, "but I'm not sure how deep it goes."

"You have hard lines around the jaw but you're beautiful anyway," said Harry.

"Those hard lines give me character. They show I'm not formless. They make me not only beautiful but interesting. I accentuate them in my make-up. They make me look carnivorous. Men like that."

"You're right, you do look a little carnivorous," said Harry. "I look good no matter in what light; I'm not sure I look interesting, though. I suppose you have to be interested in something to look interesting."

"I'm not," said Eugenie.

"Neither am I."

"Are you interested in me?"

Harry frowned. He turned away from Eugenie and surveyed the party. Everyone waved.

"Usually when I'm in a room I can tell everyone is looking at *me*. This time I can't be sure which one of us they're looking at —"

"Me," said Eugenie.

"No, I think — me," said Harry, "but I do find that interesting."

"Do you know how to love?" Eugenie asked.

"Oh, sure. I love almost everything I do. But lately I've been bored."

"I mean — a woman. Have you ever loved a woman ?"

"No."

"I've never loved anyone," said Eugenie.

"Everybody loves me," said Harry.

"I don't."

"No kidding. Well, maybe it takes a little longer with you."

"Do you love me?" she asked.

"As a matter of fact I don't. But I find you — I don't know — more or less exciting."

"I could make you love me."

"Oh sure," Harry laughed. "Listen, the way I feel these days you're lucky I find you exciting."

"Why am I exciting?"

"You remind me a little of me," said Harry.

"I made you feel closer to yourself?"

"That's right. Do I do that to you?"

"Exactly! It's the strangest feeling."

They paused and stared curiously at each other.

"Being with you is like being with me," said Harry.

"Yes, I know what you mean. However, I have more depth. But then I've lived more."

"I don't want depth. People who have it usually brood a lot."

"You are a reflection of me in a hand mirror; I am a reflection of you in a deep pool," said Eugenie.

"I'd ask you to marry me if I knew how we could live," said Harry, beginning on a new subject.

"I could continue working," said Eugenie.

"You sure you won't mind ?"

"Oh, damn." She banged a hand against her brow; an unhandsome gesture, Harry thought. "I'm supposed to be back in London tomorrow morning!"

"Oh well, then forget it," he said.

"No   to hell with it   London isn't important any more."

"A job is a job," said Harry.

"I'll find work over here," said Eugenie.

"Golly, with what you make to pay our rent and with people around to buy us our meals I don't see why we shouldn't do splendidly!"

The Blue Belles were outraged.

13.

Harry and Eugenie found a large apartment in Midtown with a mirrored lobby, a mirrored elevator, and seven comfortable rooms with mirrors on every wall. In the bedroom they installed a mirror on the ceiling that could be raised and lowered by pulleys. The mirrors in the dining room were angled around the table so that they could watch themselves eating from a variety of positions. The table itself had a mirrored surface. Though they usually dined alone, the table always seemed crowded. The largest of the bedroom mirrors had two hinged leaves that they liked to close around themselves, then, with gluttonous eyes, they revolved slowly. They spent their days looking into mirrors. They looked at themselves and at each other and at themselves looking at each other and at themselves pretending to look at each other while really still looking at themselves and at themselves making love.

In the beginning there was some difficulty with their lovemaking. Eugenie was reluctant to indulge; her only experience in its use was as a weapon.

"I don't think I can," she said.

"Sure you can," Harry assured her.

"How can I get excited? I know I won't get excited."

"Think of me."

"You're nice. But that won't do it."

"Well, what do you usually think of?"

"Hate. That's my problem. I always think of hate and it comes off very well. If I could only think of something else. Give me something that I can *use*. What do *you* think of?"

"Myself," said Harry.

"That's an idea."

She thought of herself and their first experience, though trying, was successful. After a while she became used to it, eventually finding that doing it with Harry was almost as much fun as doing it by herself.

They saw, felt, listened to, and thought of nothing but themselves. They showed home movies to themselves of themselves and held hands while they screened them. They took albums of photographs of each other and once a day pored over them; Harry inspecting his pictures, Eugenie inspecting hers. Sometimes they danced, sometimes they talked. They hated to go out anywhere; Eugenie particularly hated to go to work. Each evening she'd rise quietly so as not to disturb Harry and slip off to business. During the hours she was gone Harry felt restless and uncomfortable; a new feeling for him. It wasn't that he missed her; he missed himself when she was not there. He felt numb, erased, inexact, and with Eugenie it was the same.

"I'm no longer myself without you," she told him.

"Me too," agreed Harry.

"It's as if I'm pretending to be me. It may convince others but I know it's an act. I don't like having to act like myself. Imitations are always so sterile."

"I don't know what to do around this darn place," said Harry.

"I can hardly work," said Eugenie. "I've come to hate my job. I do it mechanically. No more pleasure. It's increased my efficiency but there used to be pleasure."

"A job is a job," chastened Harry.

"Every minute without you is a minute without both of us," said Eugenie. They went to a mirror and embraced.

They moved through their days in a state of automatic rapture. They never quarreled, they never even bickered. Their voices were extensions of their beauty; each comment was the right one, each answer was perfectly matched to the question.

Theirs was less a relationship than an orchestration. One clean line flowed between them and when they were together, its tightness took in the world.

"If it's one thing we are, it's everything," Eugenie once commented.

When they were apart the line unraveled and the world got away.

So they spent more time with each other. Eugenie went from taking occasional nights off to taking every second night off to taking every night off. They inhaled and exhaled only themselves and kept the windows shut tight so that no odor could escape. The perfume of their bodies lightened the air; it aided their breathing and improved their skin tones. They began to look luminous. Dusk was a favorite time of day; they delayed turning the lights on till the last of the day dwindled and their glowing outlines had ranged from a golden orange to a dark and burning blue. Their bodies held the color like live coals.

One day when Harry touched Eugenie his hand left a purple bruise that stayed for hours. Their skins had become too sensitive to touch. From then on they were careful not to come near each other.

"It's becoming harder and harder to look at myself," called Harry from the easy chair he had positioned in front of the bathroom mirror. "The glare is blinding."

"I know how you feel," answered Eugenie as she stared at her reflection in the coffee table. "We're becoming unreal."

"Godlike," said Harry.

"Goddesslike," corrected Eugenie.

Having established rapport, they returned to their work.

Conversation became a rarity. Several times a day, to confirm the other's closeness, one of them would mumble and then drop back into silence. Finally it was too much; it was overindulgence. Both began to feel glutted and lazy; worn down by the unwavering singularity of their lives. But neither wished to commit himself to change. So, with all the windows shut tight and the air growing clammy, they said the same things and they did the same things.

"What?" asked Eugenie after the silence of many hours.

"Never mind," said Harry. "I was about to say something but then I remembered having said it before."

"I feel that I've said everything before," said Eugenie.

"Let's try to say things that nobody has ever said!"

"Grasnyk," said Eugenie.

"Frmploh," answered Harry.

" Bzmpssrk," said Eugenie.

"Klmnx ogtvpx," said Harry.

"Rplxtphrskprdznk Opsklmxe," said Eugenie.

After several days, this too became tiresome.

"What can two people do with each other when neither of them is being destructive?" asked Eugenie one day in frustration.

"We can sit," offered Harry.

"I've had sitting. I'd rather lie than sit."

"Then we can lie," said Harry.

So they went to bed and didn't get up for three weeks. They slept, they dozed, they daydreamed, they yawned, they played but did not listen to the radio, they got up for water, they twisted themselves in the sheets, they saw how close they could move to each other without touching, they shifted sides, they curled, stretched, turned over, made up songs, got depressed.

They tried games.

"Now close your eyes. Now which part of my body am I touching?"

"Your eyes."

"No."

"Your mouth."

"No."

"Is it upper, middle or lower region?"

"Middle."

"Is it upper middle, middle middle or lower middle?"

"Lower middle."

"The navel."

"That's not the lower middle, that's middle middle."

For a time this game managed to keep them amused.

One day, Eugenie's stomach, for the first time in her memory, rumbled. The next day, for the first time in his life, Harry hiccoughed. The air closed in around them, pushing their breaths back into their bodies and out again every which way. Finally they were forced to open the windows.

"I know what's the matter with me," Eugenie decided. "I'm too white."

"You can't be too white," said Harry. "White is beautiful."

"I'm bored with white. I need a suntan."

"Sun dries out the skin."

"I'll feel like a new woman with a suntan."

"I like me fine the way I am," grumbled Harry.

It was their first quarrel.

They both knew what was coming. They feared it as much as they welcomed it.

"We're going to die in here," Harry began.

"That's why I wanted to get out in the sun. Things change out in the sun."

"I don't feel like myself any more," said Harry.

"I know what you mean."

"I don't even feel like the two of us," he added.

"Nothing. Blah. That's how I feel," Eugenie said.

"Blah. Yes, blah," Harry agreed.

"I feel that a net has descended over me," continued Eugenie.

"I feel as if I'm in a slow-motion movie," said Harry.

"Or a beautiful, serene still photograph," said Eugenie.

"Paralyzed," lamented Harry.

"Dead."

"We're no good this way," said Harry.

"No good to ourselves," agreed Eugenie.

"I have to be alone for a while," said Harry.

"I've been offered a freelance assignment in Acapulco — a head of state."

"Sounds wonderful for you," said Harry.

"That way I can get my suntan and make some money at the same time. I don't think I can afford to turn it down."

"A job is a job," said Harry.

He helped her pack.

"You don't have to take me to the airport," said Eugenie.

"I'll say goodbye here," Harry said, "carrying her bags to the elevator.

When he returned to the apartment, he wandered through each room slowly and thoughtfully. After fifteen minutes he began to whistle. Ten minutes later he began to talk: "Harry! Hello, Harry! How are you, Harry? What are you going to do today, Harry? Where have you been? It's been a long time, Harry!"

Then he showered, shaved, dressed very carefully, and took himself to an expensive restaurant.

14.

"Guess who's around town again?" Belle Mankis muttered to her colleagues after their escorts had been sent from the table for cigarettes. The Blue Belles made unpleasant noises.

"Don't I know," said Viola Strife, "I saw him last night at the Four Seasons with Brenda Washburn."

"She's through," said Belle Mankis.

"I saw him at '21' with Lucretia Pyle," said Naomi Peel.

"She's through," said Belle Mankis.

"He was at La Fonda when I was there," said India Anderbull. "He was with Grace Ventricle."

"She's through," said Belle Mankis.

"We saw him at Pavilion with Alice Light," reported Arlene Moon. The table fell grimly silent.

"Who?" asked Georgette Wallender.

It was a new Georgette who had returned from the rest home. Her eyes shone, her hair sparkled, the deep lines in her face added a knowing strength to the naïve strength that had been there before. Having been made to suffer, she had met suffering squarely and converted it to her needs as she had everything and everyone until Harry. Suffering, she realized, had cleansed her soul; pried open a heart that had been selfishly turned inward. She knew that she had used Harry; cunningly and mercilessly used him, confusing her determination for control for her determination to love. Learning this had been a bonus; a real plus. It added a number of new points to her character. She saw herself as warm where she had once been cold; ready to give — to love — to not be loved in return — to suffer. She had made suffering work for her and knew its positive aspects. She was now suffering's partisan, its devoted defender, regretting only that so many shallow years had been wasted before learning its punishing truths. Why, she wondered, had she been allowed to come so far in the world whose depth was beyond her, whose painful beauty she had only minimally begun to understand? Had her glibness really been that effective; or was it that her friends were too bland to notice, too much like the old Georgette to be further trusted? She viewed them with growing suspicion.

Only Harry had gauged her correctly; by rejecting her he had proved the soundness of his taste. His incorruptible spirit had scented the sham in her lectures, the lies in her easy truisms. Harry had rejected her and now she too had rejected her. Gone was the old Georgette; in her place stood *Georgette*! If only Harry could see her; how surprised he would be! His sharp eye would know her newness in a flash; that she no longer wanted to use him; that she had grown free of wanting to take; that now her life was all give. Give. Give. Give. Give. Give.

"Oh, Georgette!" Harry cried in her dreams a thousand times a day. "you have crossed over the mountain and are mine!"

Sometimes she let him take her. Other times she turned away. "No, Harry, you are all love and I am cheap self-pity. Perhaps someday with even more suffering my selfishness will die and I will be ready to come to you.

But for now — " and her dark figure slipped unseen into the night.

She had dreams where Harry followed her into hiding, bursting into the grimy, black closet, lit by a single candle, that had been her home for many years.

"I am old. What do you want with me?" she cried, covering her face with a threadbare shawl to hide the age that had grown there.

"We are both old," said Harry, removing her hands with his hands, a tear matching her tear running down his cheek. "It is time we went home."

She knew that none of this could ever be. Too much life had come between them. Harry was married and separated — she had heard that. Now he was undoubtedly off on some new happiness. What right had she to intrude? Turn up like a bad penny? A forgotten page? With all her vaunted suffering was she still not his inferior? Was it her right to inflict her sin-scarred soul on his sinless one? No, she decided, there could be nothing in it but misery for both of them. The maturing woman in her advised her to remember Harry only as the experience that set her life free; to go on from there to *new* experiences, to new and final love. The suffering woman in her accepted the advice. She would never see Harry again. She rang his downstairs bell to tell him.

15.

Georgette was always articulate in moments of crisis. She spent the evening smoking lightly, crossing and uncrossing her legs in a relaxed manner, and drinking hardly at all. She began by explaining to Harry why they must never see each other again. It seemed to go well. She listened to the even sound of her voice and remarked to herself, "My, it's going well. It's going awfully well."

Harry actually seemed to be paying attention. It took several hours and when she was through they went to bed.

The next morning she felt empty. Harry was gone, having left a note that said he was sorry they couldn't see each other any more and that he had enjoyed their friendship. The tone of the note was wrong. She recalled the previous evening with embarrassment; it hadn't gone well at all. She had ended by giving a lecture, just as in the old days! How could she expect Harry to understand why they could no longer see each other unless she showed him the new Georgette he could no longer see? She waited till he came home to begin over again.

But it went just as badly. "Oh, God," she thought, "he's winding his watch!"

Harry was tired. She was tired. They went to bed.

She stayed three weeks trying to explain. She cleaned house, cooked dinner and, during the odd moments when Harry was there, talked about feeling and giving and communication and contact. The further away Harry drifted, the more she blamed herself. She was not getting through.

He was always polite. When he brought dates home he said, "Stick around if you want to." She always did, patiently waiting for the girl to go home so that she at last could properly tell him why they must never see each other again.

Each new morning she left his bed sated and defeated. She tried telling herself that this was another rich experience, another triumph of suffering. But she was not suffering and she knew it. She was eroding. Harry ignored her conversation completely; he barely noticed her in bed. That he satisfied her nonetheless had become degrading.

"There's only one way I can get my point across about how suffering has changed me, Harry."

"Terrific," said Harry.

"I am going to demonstrate to you that I'm not the selfish, compulsive, opportunistic Georgette you used to know."

Harry was thumbing through a men's fashion magazine and did not answer.

"I am going to prove that I'm not an egoist. I am going to kill myself."

But Harry was too involved selecting a fall wardrobe to respond. Later they went to bed.

The mature woman in Georgette told her that suicide was the only answer. Harry would certainly get her message if she killed herself. The sensitive soul she had failed to reveal would at last be made known to him. Her death would show what he might not have lost had she only found a way to present her facts more cogently.

"I am going to kill myself, Harry. It's the only way," she told him one morning. "I thought it out. Don't try to dissuade me."

"You're crazy!" Harry laughed. At moments like these he genuinely enjoyed her.

"I'm a failure."

"You're a crazy kid."

He played in bed with her all day. Talk like that charmed him thoroughly.

Her attempt to commit suicide was becoming as embarrassing as her attempts to leave Harry. Each morning she lay in bed with new ambition, Harry's warm body beside her, a further thrust to the completion of her plan. She was going to rise from bed and then she was going to do it — really do it. Her period of indecision was past. She was finally in the mood. Very soon now she was going to rise from bed and then she was going to do it. By nightfall she was back in bed — waiting to see if Harry would come home. Would he be alone? Would he have a date? Would it be proper to tell him her plans while the date was there or should she wait for her to leave?

One night, while having nothing better to do, she wrote a suicide note:

Well, Harry, I told you and you didn't believe me. By the time you read this note I will be dead. I do not ask that you cry for me. I don't deserve your tears. I only ask that you absorb the lesson that I am trying to teach: that I must die because I have failed to make contact. I have tried but I am not skilled enough to make you know my feelings. You have never really seen me, Harry. You have never looked. But it is not your fault, really. I was never there to be seen. I don't mean to criticize.

I have suffered but I cannot communicate my suffering. However I try it comes out as self-pity. I wonder as I sit here if this is the way it is with all of us. There must be something more than words to express the emotions that the best of words don't seem to be able to. I do not know. I'm only asking.

What is almost as beautiful as you, Harry? A baby. And why? Because it is new. Because it is virginal and innocent and interested in nothing but itself. A newly minted anything has beauty, and this is a baby's beauty. But the moment life begins to touch the baby it loses its look of newness; it loses its innocence. It grows away from perfection.

Life is an abrasive. The more you come in contact with it the more it uglies you. To make contact is to uglify. To give is to leave yourself open, to leave yourself open is to be hurt. Love, true love, is the act of taking all these negative factors and turning them into gold. To make ugliness beauty; to make suffering joyous; to make giving receiving.

People who do not make contact do not live. They only exist. Existing isn't living, Harry. We must open our hearts to others if we are to live. I have tried and failed. If you are ever to be happy you must try and succeed. Give, Harry. Give, Give, Give — or die.

I kill myself to teach you this lesson. Do not try to read any other reason into my death. My career has never been as successful. My finances are in perfect order. I have many friends who love me. No, Harry, the reason I give my life is to help you to give yours.

I ask you not to feel sorry. I teach more by dying than I ever could by living. I suppose in my heart I have always been an educator.

With Feeling,

Georgette

It was rough — but it was only a first draft.

By writing the note she knew she had crossed over a line. The myth had taken form; it was now quite clear she was going to do it. She even had a plan: she would take a room in a hotel (the shape of the room came alive before her), wait till it was early morning and the streets were deserted — and then she would jump. It was inexorable. The tug of tragedy sucked her toward her final future. She flushed with a sense of Greek drama and waited for Harry to tell him the news and read him her letter. While waiting she corrected the spelling and punctuation and started on a final draft.

It was three in the morning when she finished; and Harry was still not home. She knew he would not be back at all. It left her the rest of the night with nothing to do. She reread her letter a number of times. The first dozen times she cried; the last few times it bored her. Her sense of purpose was diminishing. She tried television but nothing was on. She made herself a sandwich. She paced. She searched the apartment for cigarettes. After coffee she decided that if she was ever going to kill herself she had better do it now.

It was past four o'clock before Georgette found a decent hotel. She was shocked and annoyed: how must New York seem to out-of-town visitors? Sullen desk clerks, avaricious bellhops, dark, urine-colored corridors with colorless carpeting leading into colorless rooms; windows that opened on other windows; buildings so close to one another that had she jumped off one she couldn't have fallen — she would have had to slide. Disgraceful!

She had a clear idea of what she needed; a room that was not just a hotel room but a transition chamber. In it she would move from one world into another. That called for high ceilings with many curtains, powder blue walls, a crystal chandelier, early American furniture (an old writing desk in the corner) exquisite hand-loomed rugs — and no television. She required a view of a park from wall-high windows that opened easily and did not make one stoop to climb out. She needed a comfortable ledge to balance on; she planned to balance for a long time and do nothing but stare out at the park and feel life rush at her, more vivid than it was because of her leaving it.

The room she finally settled on was a compromise. It looked out on Bryant Park and had traditional furniture. It had television but at Georgette's insistence the management agreed to remove it in the morning. Georgette said she didn't care about the morning, she wanted it out now. The night clerk said he had no one on hand to do the job and she would have to wait. Georgette said she would move it herself.

"Do as you like but you will be billed if there is any damage," said the night clerk. Then he asked if she had luggage.

Georgette said no.

"Then I must ask you to pay in advance," said the night clerk with quiet satisfaction.

"How much?" asked Georgette.

"Twenty-five dollars," said the night clerk.

"But I'm not even going to use the room all night," said Georgette.

The night clerk stared patiently through her.

"I'll come back with luggage," she said. She was damned if she'd be taken advantage of.

One thing was certain — she couldn't return to Harry's for a suitcase. What if he were home? She wasn't sure she'd leave. Nor could she return to her own apartment. She hadn't been there in a month and to go now — to move through her rooms, go through her closets, feel her dresses, say goodbye to her jewelry — and then to find something out of order, something she had always meant to change, knowing she couldn't die without changing it, getting down to work and in the heat of activity letting this, her grandest moment, slip away; because a hem needed fixing, a waist needed taking in, or a seam needed stitching.

Enemies of her suicide lurked everywhere: the night clerk — her closets — herself. She was not going to truckle under. It had become a matter of principle. She would not go home and she *would* get into that damned hotel without paying. She would *die* without paying. Let the night clerk explain *that* to his superiors!

She called Belle Mankis.

"Georgette, darling! Where in the world have you been?"

"Belle, I'm sorry — did I wake you?"

"No, we're all here playing 'Lifeboat.' Get over here at once!"

"I can't, Belle. I have to ask you for a favor."

"Good God, darling — anything!"

"Can I borrow a suitcase?"

"Dear heart, are you all right?"

"Please, Belle, I can't explain but I need a suitcase right away and I just don't have the energy left to go over to your place and get it. I'd be desperately grateful if you'd bring it to me at the Forty-second Street entrance of the library. Please, Belle."

"Is this a new game? Sounds marvelous! Where in God's name have you been hiding?"

"Will you bring it, Belle? Please? Will you bring it?"

Belle Mankis and the Blue Belles descended on the Public Library in a squad of taxis; singing, laughing, having quite a time for themselves. They bounced Georgette between them; surrounded her in a wall of gossip, asked many pointless questions and demanded that she join them on the weekend for skiing.

"You must come Saturday," said Belle. "Everybody you know! You will come. You must. You will. It's settled. Not another word. It's settled."

"Where is the suitcase?"

"Oh my God!" said Belle. "I *knew* you wanted something!"

At five-thirty in the morning Georgette found a luggage shop on a darkened section of Thirty-ninth Street. She hurled a brick through the window, grabbed a set of matched luggage and ran.

Fifteen minutes later she registered at the hotel and had her bags taken to her room. She gave the bellboy a dollar and he helped her carry the television set into the hall. The dawn was rising and it left her less time to dawdle than she wanted. She struggled over whether she should call Harry for a last goodbye. She dialed his number and got the answering service. They told her to wait a minute. Georgette hung up. She tried to think of other people to call. She couldn't. She went to the bathroom and washed her face and combed her hair.

By the time she stepped on the ledge it was morning. She looked across to Bryant Park trying to choose a spot to fix her eye on when she jumped. She picked the clear outline of an elm tree. It looked peaceful; it looked complete. As the sun rose the tree's outline sharpened, staring at Georgette as hard as Georgette stared at it. She tried to make the tree look like Harry, so that it would be Harry she would to be jumping toward. But the tree stayed a tree. She flirted with it, swaying toward the edge, then stopping short. She waited for the growing morning traffic to notice her. She waited for cries of, "Stop! Stop! You have too much to live for!" She waited for the cops and the priest to crawl out on the ledge and talk to her. And she would say, "Bring Harry." And Harry would be brought awash in tears, pleading with her, begging her, crying — actually crying. "I read your note, Georgette. It was the most beautiful letter I've ever read. It made me understand everything. And it is more than just a letter! It is *literature!*"

She came back to life feeling ashamed. The morning wind chilled her. "I wish I knew what I really wanted to do," she moaned as a gust of wind whipped around the corner of the building and she let it lift her off the ledge.

16.

Harry never read much. Georgette's note lay around the apartment for a week before Gladys Friend, a girl he had over to clean, found it as she swept the litter from the breakfast table.

"Do you want this note, Harry?" she asked.

"What is it?"

"I don't know. Do you want it?"

"Harry took the note from her hand and read it.

"Georgette," he remembered; "I guess I haven't heard from her in months."

"You've certainly heard from me, Harry," said Gladys Friend, picking the note from his hand. They went to bed and Harry forgot about the note until he found it raveled in the sheets the next morning.

"Crazy Georgette," he thought. For a few moments he almost felt guilty. "Crazy Georgette," he said fondly. "She said I couldn't make contact. I feel guilty, don't I? Well, isn't that contact?"

He congratulated himself on his refutation of her argument. If she had indeed killed herself to help him find emotion then she had not died in vain. Harry was pleased with himself for the rest of the day.

But mixed with the pleasure was a reaction he was unable to identify. It hid aloofly within him resisting the surface; a new feeling, familiar not because he had ever experienced it but because he had either read about it or been told about it or at some time been aware of its presence in others. It came and went; Harry could not focus on it and this angered him. It made him feel less than himself, as if that were possible. He felt doubt. And that, he suddenly realized, was the feeling! Doubt! Self-doubt! Insecurity!

Harry had always accepted the fact that everyone loved him; it was the cornerstone of his life. But would a person who truly loved him voluntarily remove herself from the scene? What if he had further use of her? Could anyone so casually dismiss his needs?

At last he saw the lie in Georgette's suicide. She hadn't done it for him. She had done it for herself. She hadn't given; she had taken. It was not a love-filled sacrifice but an act of petty selfishness, an act of vindictive egotism! She hadn't thought of Harry when she took gas or went out the window or did whatever it was she did. She had thought only of Georgette, of Georgette's wants, of Georgette's moods, of Georgette's problems! She was spoiled rotten! It made Harry sick to think of it.

If Georgette could kill herself then so could any of the others. They could just pick themselves up and say to hell with Harry and go die! They could do what *they* wanted to do, not what Harry wanted them to do. And if that much were true, how could he be sure that anyone really cared for him at all? All those gifts, all those declarations, all that daily round of adoration took on a sour smell. He wasn't being given love! He was being robbed of love! Sucked dry! He stared hostilely at Gladys Friend as she slept smugly beside him. He was being *used*. Insecurity cracked like a whip through his body.

He studied the sleeping Gladys. What was she smiling at? What was she thinking? If she were a separate person she had separate ideas. She had her own personality. She probably even came from a family. Harry tried to remember if Georgette had a family. Nothing came to him. He tried to remember her face. He couldn't. He had never looked at her. He turned away from Gladys and closed his eyes. What color hair did she have? Blond, no, brunette, no — he checked. Her hair was brown. Well, he was close.

He felt like a lost child in a strange city. Who were these strangers out there who had talked to him of love and lied to him? How could he find out? He couldn't ask; he no longer trusted anyone to give an honest answer. He would have to be devious, indirect, learn as much as he could through other, less crucial questions. It was a job that required careful observation and evaluation; and it could be accomplished in only one way — Georgette's way: he would try to make contact.

These thoughts did not come all at once. They struck in tortured droplets — a few each day. He tried to keep them in order, define them one by one and store them for further use. But he had no background to work with. Insights trickled through and toured unorganized through his awakening imagination.

He attempted to shift focus; to force his attention on the world outside him. But it only held for a moment and then snapped back like a spring. He thrilled Gladys Friend by asking her questions.

"Do you have a job or something?" He was determined to make a breakthrough.

"How wonderful of you to ask! I'm a writer, actually."

He'd do it little by little. Make contact at least once a day.

"Do you have a job or something?"

"Yes, a writer. I'm a writer."

He'd begin by pretending to have an interest in people. The first week for two hours a day; the second week, four hours a day — in time perhaps it would become a habit.

"How long have you been working there?"

"Where? I work here. In the next room. You must have heard me type."

What did Gladys really feel? How could he get inside her? What was she out to get from him?

"Listen, what exactly do you do? Do you have a job or something?"

"I write. I'm a writer."

"Give," Georgette had written. "Give, give, give — or die."

But to whom was he to give? The horny-handed takers with their falsified love? Give to them openly what they had already stolen on the sly? His friendship, his company, his goodwill — well, why not? It seemed that they were going to get it anyway. Harry could not help smiling at that; at least he had kept his sense of humor.

"I'm a writer. I'm a writer," said Gladys Friend.

The more he tried to make contact the more confused his relations became. Gladys Friend turned wary; his other women acted shy. Those who once moved silkily toward him began to jerk, stumble, twitch and fall. No one knew what the trouble was; their faces drew tight with fear as they waited for Harry's next question.

And the results proved disappointing. He felt no more than he did before. In the past he had seen people as tools; now he saw them as strangers and enemies. He did not consider this progress.

In the midst of his gloom a telegram came from Eugenie: "Arrive 7 A.M. at Idlewild. You needn't meet me."

17.

Harry ran from the apartment. "Where's a flower shop? Where's a flower shop?" he asked the doorman to his building and having the one next door indicated he rushed in and ordered roses.

With his arms full he staggered back into the apartment and searched all the closets for a vase. There wasn't one. He ran out again and found a store that sold him a dozen vases. He positioned the vases around the living room and in each one he placed a fistful of roses. He stung his fingers repeatedly. Only when the act was completed was he struck by the enormity of what he had done. He had bought his wife a present.

He had never given a present to anybody. A warm flush of shyness crept over him and then — joy. Joy in its full, familiar flavor but larger than he remembered it; brighter, more exciting, more true. Joy and with it the first tremor of a new beginning. Here, without effort or plan, Harry had given a room full of flowers. He had crossed a continent. He had given!

And it was just as Georgette had said; no feeling could rival this one. He stood in the center of the room and revolved slowly, letting his gaze sweep from vase to vase. He was one with the vases and one with the flowers inside them. Was this how it was with other people? This surrender to sudden communion? A shiver of ecstasy excited his toes and made him want to dance. He looked at the flowers and felt contact. The flowers made him think of giving and giving made him think of Eugenie to whom he had given and having given to Eugenie he saw that Eugenie would give to him and the two of them would give, give, give, to each other — because in the end they were one. One with the flowers, one with the vases, one with each other. And there lay the secret; the beauty of giving was that it was always returned.

And though he did not feel love he knew that too must come. He had taken the first step and had made contact. And making contact had taught him the meaning of communication: everybody giving all he had and taking all he could.

He stood in the center of the room whirling faster. The mirrors everywhere dozened his flashing image — flawless and beautiful — but Harry did not notice. He saw only the singing red circle of roses. He had given.

The next morning he woke up with a pimple on his nose.

PART THREE

THE
LOVE
MONSTER

1.

It wasn't there. It wasn't there and even if it were there it was bound to heal and disappear in a day. Or two days. Certainly no more than two days. He examined himself in the dark, tightly touching the part of him which, because of its discrepancy with the rest, was the center of all interest at the moment: the pimple. His hand, his warm, pliant, soft, and beautiful hand with an outside like down and an inside like velvet, set to rest on his forehead (cool, noble, molded in perfection) and slid judiciously down across perfectly formed eyes, perfectly formed cheeks (smooth and hairless), across to a firm, responsible chin, up to a mouth that sank deep, thrust forward, lay still, came alive, changed with the light of day or a turn of mood — and each change its own cameo of rightness, of justification for the whole — and swooping down toward the mouth, meeting it with an avenging passion: the villain nose. Perfect at its root, thrilling in its concourse and traitorous at its end: the pimpled tip. It saluted redly, becoming the starting-point of Harry's body, the diameter of his circle, the point of purchase from which his past dropped away and his future clung despairingly.

Facts unpleasant to face are best faced thorough avoidance — that was

Harry's philosophy. There was no pimple. He would close his eyes and throw it away from his face. He whistled, hummed and chanted the nonexistent hump into nonexistence. Harry looked upon himself as a graced body, a metaphysical principle. He had floated astrally through his childhood without hives, his adolescence without acne, his summers without mosquito bites, his winters without chapped lips. Nothing — no mark, no bruise, no scab, no inflammation, no oiliness, no dryness, no dandruff, no whitehead, no blackhead, no ulcer, no chancre — nothing, until the pimple, had separated his body from its dogmatic perfection. In metaphysics there is no room for pimples.

He eliminated it from the present. It became a shameful episode in his past, not to be discussed, a black sheep in the family. Something — but who can remember what — was once awry, but that was long ago and now everything was fine again.

As much as possible he avoided his mirror. But he could not keep his hands from his face. And each touch gave the lie to his self-deception.

For a month after Eugenie left him he remained indoors. He had no idea where the time disappeared. He would turn around and the morning was gone, sit down and the afternoon was over, muse about and it was bedtime. Had he or had he not eaten dinner? He often retired without knowing.

He didn't blame Eugenie; he blamed his stupid imperfection. Marriage was a contract and a violation of that contract a sudden change in one of the partners — was ample reason for its cancellation. Eugenie had come home to him extraordinarily beautiful — thus fulfilling her part of the contract. Harry greeted her at the door with a handful of roses.

Eugenie ignored the roses, "Hold the elevator," she called at the operator who was wheeling out her luggage. "You've got a pimple on your nose,

Harry."

"I'm dying to hear all about your trip," said Harry.

"A small, ugly, red pimple."

"I bet you have millions of stories to tell," said Harry.

"I think it's growing. Hold the elevator."

Harry shoved the roses at her. Eugenie recoiled.

"What the hell are these things — what am I supposed to do with them?"

"They're some kind of flower. I'm giving you a present." Half the roses fell through his fingers to the floor.

Eugenie glared. "You never had to give me anything before. Hold the elevator!"

Harry reached for her arm. The rest of the roses fell. "Can't we even talk?"

"You're whining, Harry. I never heard you whine before." An old look clicked into Eugenie's eyes. She turned toward the elevator.

Harry trailed after her, "When are you coming back?"

"I have a million things to do."

"Dinner? How about dinner?"

"Call me," she said, and stepped into the car.

"Where will you be?" Harry asked as the door started shut.

"I'm washing my hair," said Eugenie and the elevator went down.

"What time shall I call?" Harry asked the elevator door.

So it was over. A woman had rejected him. At first he found nothing startling about it. If he were a woman and had come back from two months work in Acapulco to find her husband with a pimple on his nose, he would also reject him. But, after a time, when he was able to face the fact of the pimple, admit that it was there and that all the powders and salves he administered only made it bigger, did he see that a rejection from even a woman of Eugenie's calibre was, and still should have been, unprecedented.

No matter what Eugenie said it could not honestly be described as ugly. If a pimple could ever be beautiful then this was that pimple: perfect in its roundness, rose-like in its redness — a masterpiece of a nose sore. It marred Harry's perfection but did not subtract from his beauty. His beauty now took on a sombre note. The pimple aged Harry. Joined him to the world. Most women would have said, "Oh, that poor little pimple. Oh, that darling little pimple!" and begged to stay over in order to nurse it.

But Eugenie, like Harry, was not of the world. Their values concerning perfection were identical. The knowledge that others would not reject him as Eugenie had drove him not toward them but further away. His desire to learn to give collided with his sorry estimate of those to whom he would be giving: the non-people-non-interesting, non-caring, non-feeling, non-perceptive.

"But surely," he told himself in his determination to believe, "there must be some perception in the world. Maybe I'm being too harsh. Maybe I underestimate people. Maybe they *will* reject me."

That night, in order to find out, he went to a party.

2.

Every Thursday Seth and Tessa Wainscot had a party for their friends. It commenced with dinner for twelve at seven-thirty, post-dinner guests arriving from nine-thirty thereafter. The guest lists were combed out of an index of the conversational elite: from the universities, from the arts, from the sciences and, on labor evenings, from the bowels of industry. Tessa Wainscot had literary evenings, dance evenings, theatre evenings, peace evenings, and evenings where the interests of her guests were as varied as their fashionably clashing opinions.

Her husband Seth was, as Tessa proudly put it, on sabbatical from academia, having once taught a course in marketing at N.Y.U. If Tessa was the creator of their evenings, Seth was their bookkeeper. His small chalk-colored head bobbed on his shoulders like a loose part, nodding at conversational points, murmuring "mmm" in agreement or "mmm, mmm" in disagreement, grading and filing away for future reference the debating points of his guests so that he was able to score their importance to subsequent evenings: "Ah, Professor Diddendet made an A last week in nuclear games theory but barely deserved a C in German cinema of the 1920s."

Tessa Wainscot's money (oil, lumber, and Happee Farms White Bread) supported both her husband and her salon, but it was really her multiplicity of interests that kept the salon flourishing. Her fastidious sense of timing selected the narcotics question for discussion at the moment it was coming ripe and abruptly dismissed the anti-communist question weeks before it turned stale. She smelled the next discussable crises wafting over the horizon; a distant delectable odor. Before it was ready to be served she had drawn up a guest list.

She was a small woman but grabby; her tiny fingers quivered with the expectation of taking hold. She strengthened her grip on her guests' hands; she dried her lips on their necks; she lost the powder from her arms on their clothing. Once she had hold of a hand she forgot she had it until a new hand came within reach and then she had two. She twirled the caught hands like lariats, using them as extensions of her arms and making conversational points with them. The only person she had never been able to touch was Harry. His occasional appearances left her emptyhanded and chastened; turning her salon into his salon, turning her house into his. She became one of the guests; a shy one moving as quietly in the background as her husband Seth; her out-of-action fingers doing impatient dance steps up and down her body.

But as Harry joined the party on this particular evening, entering the house he had never noticed to be a brownstone before, seeing the sharp, clear crowd as if a filter had been removed from his vision, hearing new sounds and registering new colors, he saw, looming out of the background, the woman he vaguely recognized as his hostess. Before he could wave hello Tessa Wainscot had both his hands up to the knuckles and was squeezing. Something had happened.

Whatever it was, it wasn't rejection. Familiarity thick as smog closed in on Harry. His back was paddled, his arms pummeled, his shoulders surrounded by heavy arms, male and female. He was touchable. And all who touched him were clear. People took shape and size in front of him. Blurs became distinct. Faces had expression, bodies had shape, people wore clothing.

But this wasn't what Harry left his room to see. He had opened his eyes to find rejection and people saw the opening and walked right in. He tried to replace the filter but it was too late. He could not keep out the touchers. He retreated and they followed. Their goodwill left him limp. His pimple had changed *everything!*

Tessa connected his hand to another hand, "Of course, you've met dozens of times. Arnold Maim, the film maker," and he did remember that somewhere, perhaps here, he had seen the soft roseate face, the pink mustache, the small, child's teeth — but the hand was gone before he could be sure and another hand was in its place.

"You've met dozens of times — Audrey Aspen, the dancer." And this face too, spare as a trimmed bone, came and went in his memory. They marched past him with insane cheerfulness, grinning with the ambition to be liked and the insinuation that dared suggest Harry was now one of them. Their grins, their hearty goodwill, their shoves and pinches drove him to the wall. How much better rejection would have been than this. Disappointment mixed with his desire to escape. The voices he had heard somewhere called after him and the bodies, so flirtingly familiar, hove into view. He could not get away and this was the crowning indignity above all others; these people were unconcerned with his wishes. But then wasn't this the sign he was looking for? A proof that he was no longer holy? It could be nothing less! Harry's interest took a tentative rise. Perhaps people had promise after all. He stared hard at them to see better, and they stared back, grinning.

In another room the speeches were in progress. Those faces not grinning at Harry were frowning at the loud voice coming through the door. The voice, Harry thought, was familiar. Had he heard it before? Why was only one man speaking? Slowly it came back to him that the event of Tessa's evening's were the speeches of her guests. He had never listened to one. With a sense of achievement he found himself curious. He followed the voice to its owner who was concluding: "You are not sheep, you are grass! Green at the tip where it looks good. And brown and muddy at the root, passively waiting to be chewed and waiting on leaders to come decide for you when you've been chewed enough and when it's time to switch from one set of jaws chewing you to a different set of jaws! Grass will go in any direction it is blown. You, my fellow Americans, are grass! Grass! Grass!"

Arguments broke out in the audience. The speaker, a man terribly familiar to Harry, viewed the gathering with surly disdain. Tessa Wainscot appeared at his side, smiled at everyone thrillingly and grabbed a number of hands to still the bickering.

"First of all," she began, "I want to thank Dr. McCandless for risking his life by coming to our den of subversion tonight!'

(Appreciative laughter)

"Dr. McCandless is the first right-winger we've had since Madame Chiang honored us with her presence so many years ago."

(Oohs and ahhhs)

"I hope it won't be your last appearance here, Doctor, nor the last hearing we will have of your interesting point of view."

(Applause. A smirk from McCandless)

"Now I know I promised you all that if you came to hear Dr. McCandless speak there would not be any collection, but he is the only right-winger most of us know and he does have to eat."

(Appreciative laughter and applause. A good-natured smile from McCandless)

"No, seriously though, Dr. McCandless is devoting all of his energies at present to raising funds for a weekly publication that will give voice to his segment of political thought. Does your publication have a title, Doctor?"

"The New Reaction."

(Good-natured applause and laughter)

"Well, I don't think I have to tell anyone here how important it is to give every voice a platform in order that the people may listen and make their own choice."

"Impotent liberals," sneered McCandless.

(Appreciative laughter)

"Well, let's all prove to Dr. McCandless that we impotent liberals — ha ha — I'm really not one myself. I honestly can't decide what I am. Sometimes I think I'm an anarcho-syndicalist —"

(Appreciative, satirical, aren't-we-all-type laughter)

"But before we all drink and have fun I know I did promise that there wouldn't be any collection speeches tonight — I hate them as much as any of you — but I'm going to go back on my word and ask you to fill out the pledge card that Dr. McCandless is passing among you —"

At which point McCandless reached Harry with a pledge card.

"Pardon me, but don't I know you from somewhere?" said Harry. "Didn't you teach me once or something?" McCandless looked up from his pledge cards and gave a little cry, "My leader!"

He threw his arms around Harry and kissed him on the lips. Tears spread over the nicotine. stains that covered his face.

"I've searched for you everywhere!" he said, running his hands along Harry. "All that I now have is yours. All that I believe stems from you!" He trembled with excitement. Bits of ash flaked from his hair and body. "You are the master and I your disciple. Once, I thought — I had the temerity to think it was the other way —" He took a handful of cigarettes from a tray and began coughing at the sight of them. Harry steadied him.

"Conditioned reflex," McCandless mumbled. "The cigarette conspiracy. They found out I was their enemy and they set out to give me cancer."

His coughing lapsed into a wheeze. He lit up and began coughing again.

"Martyrdom complex," he gasped as Harry slapped his back.

"I spent a year in prison, you know."

Harry started to say that he didn't —

"Your fault indirectly," McCandless said.

Harry started to ask why it was his —

"Not sorry for a minute of it," McCandless interposed. "History is studded with the stories of suppressed revolutionaries."

Harry started to ask —

"The Grass Roots Conspiracy. Your invention. Your creed. I took it as my own. Built a philosophy on it. Created an underground subversive network, or was about to anyway when the Congressional Committee got after me. At first they thought I was simply a patriotic front because I didn't allow Negroes to join. But then they discovered it wasn't because they were black but because they were Baptist. Most of them anyhow. Our revolution only accepted atheists.

"There are no Judeo-Christians in foxholes," he chuckled to himself wisely.

"So they hauled me before the Committee and demanded that I name names. I was mortified. We had no names. I was the only member. And I couldn't take the Fifth because I'd be risking my tenure. So I named the only names I could think of at the moment — the chairman and the rest of the Committee. They put me in jail for a year for perjury."

Harry started to say he was —

"Greatest experience of my life," continued McCandless. "It was prison that gave me time to think. I went over your speech word for word, reflecting on all its philosophic implications. You had said that man would go in whatever direction he was led regardless of the character of his leadership. You had said that men were not sheep but sheep fodder. Grass, as it were; green at the tip, muddy at the root. Green for aspiration, green for the illusion of a better life. I took that as your meaning. But muddy where it counted, muddy at the foundation. And what is mud? Because you did not say dirt. Dirt can be solid. Dirt, though dirty, can be reformed. It can grow things. It can feed man. But what can mud grow? Mud shifts in many directions. Mud *is* slime. Mud can only grow swamp grass. Mud is a haven for insects and hence, I concluded, if man is nature's greatest creation what greater insect can there be than man's soul?

"And so it was to this conclusion that you had brought me. We are mud and our souls are insects. Can you imagine the unbridled joy that burst loose in my heart? Though behind bars, I felt freer than I had ever felt in my life. I was released from the restrictions of crippling, unnatural commitment. What commitment does mud have but to slide in the direction most convenient for its passage? What commitment compels the insect but the commitment to eat for itself and exist till it dies? (I here exclude the more socially corrupt insect societies.)

"I thought only of you. You were committed to yourself and you flourished. I was committed to an ethic and I was in jail. In the adjoining cell block were all the congressmen I had accused. Every day in the prison yard they beat me up. But I didn't care. I was free!

"During my final months in prison I took the last of my savings and hired a market researcher to find out for me the direction in which the mud was going. His conclusion, after a thorough analysis including poll samplings, was that the mud flowed toward right-wing liberalism.

"But the field of right-wing liberalism was already crowded with experts who, like myself, had come over from left-wing liberalism. I could see no future in it for me. But I had to make a living. So through historical analysis I traced the trend of right-wing liberalism and saw that, quantitatively, it eventually must arrive at left-wing conservatism — or as it is known generically — the radical right. I was in luck. The right-wing had no intellectual leadership. So I set myself up in advance of the field. I became the intellectual consultant to the right; the final expert on all matters of doctrine; an arbiter of the faith and a clearing house for the suspected."

McCandless crushed Harry to him. "And it's yours, all yours!"

Harry freed himself. "But I don't believe that stuff any more. People don't have to be mud. People can learn to communicate. Mud can't communicate. People can learn to give. Can mud give? Can mud love?"

McCandless was always easily convinced by anything Harry said. "Yes, you're absolutely right. I was wrong. People can learn to communicate. You're right. Mud can't. You certainly have a solid point. Mud cannot love."

His face darkened in confusion, but then brightened again. "Wait! I am the proof of your own rejected philosophy. Look how easily I followed you. I went the way you went. I was mud!"

"But mud cannot love!" insisted Harry.

McCandless was convinced. "Yes, that is very true. What you say is true. Who has ever heard of mud loving?"

Then he grinned triumphantly. "But do people love? Or do they just love to think they love? They love to eat tuna fish sandwiches, they love to go swimming, they love to sleep late in the morning, they love to watch television. Don't you see? If the act of love can be made to function on so many disparate levels, as a scientific description, how can it exist at all?"

The reply to McCandless' question did not come from Harry but from a gaunt, light-skinned Negro who stepped furiously into their circle and shouted, "You white sons of bitches!"

A murmur of pleasure warmed the room.

"The Negro Question!" people whispered and formed a crowd around them.

"You speak of love! What love?" cried the Negro.

"Yes, yes," answered the crowd quietly.

"Hairsplitting Love! Do-Gooder Love! White Man's Love!"

"Oh yes," trilled the crowd.

The Negro, staring only at Harry, began moving in and out in a dancing crouch.

"Well, I'm here to tell you that Love's everlasting but it's not *your* Love!" and he pointed at Harry.

"No!" trilled the crowd.

"And it's not *his* Love!" He pointed at McCandless. "No!" said the crowd.

"And it's not the Love of anyone here. Not anyone! Not anyone!"

"No. No," said the crowd.

"And I'm here to tell you that Love's everlasting but you'll never know it!"

"Tell us! Tell us!" cried the crowd.

"If you're white you're all right.

If you're brown stick around.

If you're black stand back!

White Man's Love!"

"White Man's Love!" cried the white crowd, swaying in rhythm.

"Well, I'm here to tell you the only Love you know is the Love of Suppression!"

"Yes!" said the crowd.

"The Love of Intimidation!"

"Yes!" went the crowd.

"The Love of the Master knowing he *is* the Master!"

"Yes! Yes!"

"The Love of the innkeeper sending Mary to the manger with a check for the NAACP!"

"Tell us! Tell us!" writhed the crowd. And McCandless writhed with them, "Tell us! Tell us!"

But when the writhing cooled the Negro was gone and in his place stood Tessa Wainscot.

"Now I know I told all of you when I invited you here that there would be no collection speeches but I think the point of view represented by our guest, Dr. Grace, whose work with underdeveloped countries we are all so familiar with, is so compelling that I'm going to go back on my word and —"

When the Negro reached Harry and McCandless with his pledge card, McCandless, sobbing uncontrollably, handed him all of his own.

"I always leave here broke," he managed to tell Harry before collapsing in his arms.

"You probably don't want to talk to me now," said the Negro, whose name was Stanley Grace. "You probably hate me."

"Not at all," said Harry. "I tried to listen but my mind wandered. I'm not used to listening yet."

Grace grinned. He couldn't help grinning at Harry.

"I used to be a big fan of the Negro Question but I switched sides recently," said McCandless, drying his eyes.

"You white son of a bitch!" said Grace.

McCandless gave him another five dollars. Grace pocketed it and moved toward the door.

"Let's split before the Indian comes on," he said. "He comes on so hard that when he's through he's got all *my* pledge cards. "

But they were too late. A rising, peaking, dropping voice filled the room like a guilty conscience.

"You Americans" it said with a dry, sing-song chuckle. "You Americans."

N. V. Shad, the Indian diplomat, grinned knowingly from the center of the room. The crowd swallowed him instantly.

"You Americans," Shad pronounced carefully over the heads of the crowd, "you are all so preoccupied with your sense of self — yourself this — yourself that — that you scarcely have time to consider the Selves of Others."

The crowd exchanged looks of happy guilt.

"Other peoples. Other forms of government. Other philosophies of life."

"What about Kashmir?" cried a hostile drunk. "Shush," hissed the embarrassed crowd, reaching for its billfolds.

Shad smiled, "You Americans always bring up Kashmir when you wish to avoid discussing the Bomb." His eyes blinked slowly and wisely. The crowd cheered and grabbed for his pledge cards.

"Congratulations," said Stanley Grace bitterly, tears of guilt ballooning his eyes. "You know I can't cut the Bomb Question." He handed Shad all his pledge cards.

"Winner buys the drinks," said Shad, grinning wisely at Harry; and they all took a taxi to his place.

On the drive uptown Harry found the hand of Stanley Grace sliding up his knee.

"You probably don't go for black boys," said Grace in a hostile undertone.

"Actually you're very light." said Harry.

"You know what I mean," growled Grace.

"Actually, I'll try anything once," said Harry.

"You never made it with a black boy?"

"No," said Harry.

Grace looked suspicious. "You ever make it with a white boy?"

"No," said Harry, trying to remember. "I can almost definitely say I haven't."

Grace pulled his hand away. "Son of a bitch. You're all alike. Just being nice to me."

In the front of the cab, McCandless and Shad were engaged in an active discussion on the Trotskyite movement in India.

N. V. Shad lived alone in an indirectly lit Upper East Side apartment that smelled of animal skins. He kept six cats who prowled the apartment casting shadows like a horror movie. He offered his guests a selection of saris to relax in; they all declined. Shad chuckled wisely and said, "You Americans," then he served drinks.

Stanley Grace became increasingly sober with each drink. He stared sullenly at Harry. When Harry stared back, Grace grinned, stared away and tried to look sullen again. Shad took it all in with a wise chuckle, "You Americans," he said. Stanley Grace sprang from his chair and placed a bony, tanned fist under Shad's nose. "Don't call me American, man! See that skin? That's black!"

"Mine is darker," said Shad and placed his hand on Stanley Grace's.

"So is mine," said McCandless, who was quite swarthy. The three of them held hands.

"I'm very white," said Harry. "I hate the sun."

"Patronizing sons of bitches!" cried Grace, breaking free of the string of hands. "All I give you is hate and all you give me back is understanding. You think that's what I want?" He avoided looking at Harry; now was not the moment to grin.

"I don't want you mothers to love me. I know you're the enemy! You wouldn't hate me for being black so I turned communist. You insisted I turned communist because of my bitter background and you gave me more love— so I turned queer! You insisted I only turned queer because I can't fulfill my normal role in a white society and you gave me more love. So I turned junkie! You insisted I turned junkie because I never had a chance. And you gave me more love," Grace sobbed.

"Where is your White Love going to leave me? It won't let me have the power to make myself a communist, it takes away my free choice to be a queer, it robs me of the will to be a junkie. It does it all for me. Nothing left for me to do ever." He shuffled servilely across the floor. "Thank you, White Love!"

McCandless jerked to his feet; tears ran down his face and a dry, choking noise made static in his throat. "Love," he finally wailed; his voice sounded ragged with age. "What is love but a lie Man created to keep other men from destroying Him?" Stanley Grace nodded savagely.

"Love!" gasped McCandless. "What is love but a methodology to achieve a desired end by means more convenient than violence?"

"Amen," nodded Stanley Grace.

McCandless trembled with insight. "There is only one kind of love: self-love. To give to others is to take from oneself unless by giving one adds to his sense of himself. But this then is not giving but taking in the form of giving. What fun is charity without a thank-you note?"

"Baby!" cried Stanley Grace and hugged McCandless as if he were Harry.

McCandless hugged back and cried bitterly, "There is no love!"

Grace, fumbling to undo his clothing, returned the cry, "There is no love!" They stumbled in each other's arms across the floor.

N. V. Shad smiled and stroked a cat. "You Americans." He chuckled wisely and moved to a more comfortable chair.

Harry struggled to his feet feeling drugged. He was unaccountably depressed. "Well, I don't agree with any of you!" he shouted in order to be heard over the heavy breathing and the wise chuckling; and not receiving an answer he left.

3.

He had been ignored. Here he was: the one who left the party early, the one to whom no one paid attention. All the attention-paying had come from his end; the concentration; the involvement. And it hadn't been easy. When his mind drifted lazily off course he wrenched it back, forced his sights to fix and remain on McCandless, on Grace, on Shad. And where did his efforts leave him? On the street. Alone. Going home.

So added to Eugenie's rejection were the rejections of McCandless, Grace and Shad; it was a triumph of sorts but it left him with mixed feelings. The lessons being taught him were not satisfactory. McCandless' love was not the love Georgette spoke of; nor was it the love he remembered being born with: the love he carried as part of his body for all those many years. McCandless was wrong; confusing but wrong. Stanley Grace was wrong; confusing but wrong. Their answers were not appropriate to his questions. They had wasted his time.

But not totally — Harry had, after all, noticed them, reacted to them, listened to them. That certainly was not a waste. He felt one conversation closer to the world; one evening's argument nearer to the streets he walked through and the people he had to pass to reach home. He was tired when he arrived, exhausted by the complicated set of the evening; however, he obeyed the ritual of washing his face and saying goodnight to it in the bathroom mirror. The pimple flushed unchanged on his nose. But this time Harry did not see it. He was staring at the eruption of tiny blackheads that sometime during the evening had grown in full bloom on his forehead. Harry panicked.

He was in limbo. His body could only hold so much; when life seeped in, his beauty seeped out. Now neither held possession, yet the direction of his descent was obvious — unless he did something to stop it. But there was nothing to do; his piqued curiosity was not to be unpiqued. The danger was incredible.

He cold-creamed his face vigorously burning his skin with the rubbing force of his fingers. And perhaps this too was harmful. Perhaps in trying to help he had hurt; ruptured a membrane; given himself a rash; broken down the sensitive nerve endings so close to the surface of his skin. Perhaps his veins would begin to show. Harry became aware of an erratic rhythm in his head; a muted, painful throb — his first headache.

One thing was certain; he could not go on this way. Being alone, fingering his face, examining his body for new signs of decay was more than he could bear. Looking in the mirror was like baring a wound; if there could be no Harry to give peace to Harry he had to find someone else. He was forced into the street, entering it awkwardly, reluctant to go but more reluctant to remain where he was. And on the street he was driven to look — at people. They were as strange as a foreign language. He couldn't understand what made them move, what made them walk in their graceless ways, carrying their bodies like burdens, fighting themselves with every step, walking as if the act of standing were painful. Their arms fought their clothing; their legs beat out against their overhanging bodies, trying but failing to break away. Their faces showed passive regret.

Harry tried not to look. He had begun to see more than he wanted. He looked into eyes and they stared back grinning. But not from love; from lust. "There goes a great-looking man," grinned the comparison shoppers pricing him as he passed by. Their stares chipped away at him, knocking a piece off his shoulders, shortening his stride, changing the pace of his body. The tempo of other lives became tangled with his own. His walk was affected by whoever walked in front of him. He shuffled, he minced, he limped. "Are you making fun of me?" a shriveled man cried wretchedly at him. Harry discovered that he was. He was losing himself; he was becoming them. It was happening too fast and it had to stop. He could think of nothing else to do but talk to Phoebe Tigerman. She knew everything.

Harry had met Phoebe Tigerman as he had met and barely remembered so many others; various friends took him regularly to Fridays at Phoebe's, where they drank and dissected Thursdays at Tessa's. Phoebe, he remembered, sat like a small, watchful Buddha, taking little part in the conversations. But people said of her, "Phoebe knows everything," and their faith in her knowledge made them more open in front of her, as if her ability to see through them allowed them the freedom to be what she would see. Her guests sat at her feet, rooted there for the evening, except for those few occasions when Harry's appearance sent them sliding from her feet to his. Harry could not remember whether Phoebe slid with them. He really knew nothing about her except that she was ugly.

4.

Phoebe Tigerman had been touched and hurt early in life and the hurt, once inside, burned outward, distorting her child's face with its complex pain; turning it grotesque in its mute desire to banish the suffering. And heard over the strident pounding from the inside were the blows of her mother from the outside: "Don't twist your face like that, you awful thing. It will grow that way!" Obediently, her face followed Mother's advice and grew as she said it would: ugly. Each new attack, whether from inside or out, added a deeper hunger to the eyes and a profounder sadness to the mouth. Her body, too, was ugly; hard and cramped as a prize-fighter's crouch, designed to present as small a target as possible and render harmless those blows that broke through. But by the time she was complete no blow could. There came a day when she was still available to be hurt but those who had the power were dead. After that everyone who followed was like a lightweight. She blossomed in the knowledge of her safety. Other knowledge followed. She had a sure instinct for people, grown out of her childhood reconnaissance of them. In studying to find where the next blow would come from she found, too, the vulnerable spots for her own blows and, knowing both, she knew everything. She knew people.

Her reputation developed quickly: "Phoebe knows everything." Pilgrimages were made to her thick sandaled feet. Friends came to her like soldiers home from war: no further need to bluster or protest, just a warm fire and a soft bed. In visiting Phoebe they left their color outside: the spirit that made them loud or quiet, respected or hated. First they talked to each other and became one and then they listened to Phoebe and became anonymous.

Her face softened as her security grew. Age took away its rawness, consolidating each grotesque feature into a strikingly sculpted whole. A glow of beauty hung like a nimbus around her ugliness. She never married because she had no urge to destroy.

When Harry arrived at her apartment, having walked up the four flights with the thick smell of foreign cooking oversweetening the hall he found the usual number of people at her feet — but this time they did not slide over to his. He was not surprised but he saw that Phoebe was, and for some reason this drew him to her.

"Get out," he said to her guests. He saw that he still had enough authority to make them go. They grinned as they left. Harry noticed in Phoebe's mirror that the face they grinned at was beginning to lose its hair.

They stared at each other for a short while. Finally Phoebe said, "Did you bring a bottle?"

"No," said Harry.

"My guests usually bring a bottle. I don't have any money."

"You don't have to serve me," said Harry.

"But I like to have something to drink," said Phoebe.

"Didn't they bring bottles?" asked Harry, referring to the recently departed.

"Those were their bottles," said Phoebe. "It's important to have the feeling that you brought your own."

"People usually bring me things."

"We'll forget about it this time," said Phoebe. "What are you drinking?"

"Pernod."

Phoebe brought out a bottle. They drank quietly. Neither had anything to say.

"I only know women with money," Harry said at last. "How come you don't have any?"

He had forgotten his reason for being there.

"My grandfather left me a trust fund of millions," said Phoebe. "When I was a little girl my parents kept telling me that they were all I had and that the only reason anybody else would love me was for my money. So when I reached the age of eighteen and control of the money came into my hands I gave it all away. I didn't want to confuse the question of love. I wanted to be loved for myself or not at all."

She sipped her drink slowly.

"The next day my parents left me."

"Boy, that's a great story!" said Harry appreciatively. "That should be in a column." He wanted to tell an anecdote of his own but he was not used to the politer forms of conversation that centered on matters other than himself. After a pause he said, "Things are working out lousy for me." He waited for her to explain why.

"They come to me for insights and toss them down like alcohol," said Phoebe..

"Well, what are you going to do?" said Harry.

"I don't help anybody," Phoebe said.

"You know everything," Harry told her.

Phoebe nodded. "It's true. I give brilliant dissertations. People think I change their lives. I don't change anything but their topics of conversation."

"Change mine," said Harry provocatively.

"Don't flirt with me!" she said sharply. She didn't grin. Harry realized he had been flirting.

"People have been coming to me for years. Not one of them has ever changed. Each visit I give them an insight that they can add to their list of other insights. That's why they think I'm a saint."

"People say you know everything," Harry insisted.

"I don't try to help them," said Phoebe, "so they know they can trust me."

Harry felt that he had been let in on a great secret. He stayed fifty minutes and left buoyant with new insights. Only when he tried to pin them down did he realize that his own problems hadn't been mentioned. He looked in the mirror and saw that his hair was now thinning rapidly.

He saw Phoebe again the next morning. After driving her visitors out, he gave her a bottle of gin. Then he took his place at her feet.

"You didn't tell me anything yesterday," he accused.

"I never tell anybody anything. Thanks for the gin."

"How am I supposed to know where I'm to go next if you don't help me?" he asked, feeling cheated.

"I can't help you," said Phoebe. "My field is insights."

Harry sighed unhappily and waited for her to proceed. She poured them both gin.

"I prefer Pernod," said Harry.

"You brought gin," said Phoebe. She handed him a glass.

"I used to be beautiful," said Harry. "This morning I woke up with bags under my eyes." He looked at her pleadingly. She was small, growing larger. "Once all I had was me and that seemed enough. Now nothing seems enough."

"What do you want me to tell you?" asked Phoebe.

Harry had trouble getting the words out. "How do you learn to make contact?" he finally asked, feeling the utter inadequacy of the question.

Phoebe's eyes receded. "In the beginning," she began, "all living creatures were one-celled. All natural and subnatural processes were provided for within themselves. They even reproduced within themselves. Not by eggs, not by spermatozoa, but by the fission of the body into two or more individuals. Of that I am fairly convinced."

Harry chuckled. "Even men and women?" He had her there.

"Out of whose rib was Eve created?" Phoebe asked. "Adam and Eve were one-celled organisms — the first of their kind to go against the laws of nature. Eve's sin was not deflowering the tree of knowledge but deflowering Adam. Eve's sin was incest. And you and I are her abnormal progeny.

"And how hard we have tried to find our way back to our original state. The record of history is the sum total of man's frustrated efforts to return to a state of oneness. We are maladjusted protozoa, Harry — one-celled animals raised in a society with a multi-celled ethic. Man has forgotten his origins but historic memory sends him in a frenzied search for them. He can not admit it because he does not know what it is that he is searching for — so he invents substitutes: he searches for the messiah; he searches for the holy grail; he searches for Isolde, Eurydice, Juliet, the big money, the lost chord, the cure for cancer, world peace. All this empire building, all this lovemaking, all this meaningful relating going on around us is the hungry search to find a way back to what you have had all your life, Harry, and what I have now. One-celledness. That is why we are irresistible. We are seen as solid, secure, whole, and complete — what others go to bed with each other for and still find lacking. Lovemaking is a lost search for the other half of one's self. The selection of a mate is the final surrender of that search.

"So, settling for frustration in his own life, man must destroy the lack of frustration in the lives of others. Children are born as one-celled as you and me; so the parents' first step is to reorder the child's concern for only itself to a guilty concern for only the parents. And once all reminder of oneness is destroyed in their children they fall upon us living, healthy, grown-up reminders. They sit at our feet because we are perfect but our perfection goads them. So they set out to destroy us in the only way they can justify their own lives; they must change our image to their image; they must change our values to theirs. They tell me to come out of my shell yet it is to my shell they so willingly pay homage. They tell you to make contact with others while they strive only to make contact with themselves.

"Don't fall for their message, Harry. Don't believe a word they say. They do not know it but they are demons."

5.

But, demons or not, they had him. He was sickened by the thought of it and fully aware of the horrible truth implicit in Phoebe's warning. But he could not resist the pull to the abyss; he had come too far to go back. He had even forgotten what it meant to go back. To what? That other life without pain? He was willing to try; but where would he begin? He bought dark glasses to blot out other people and return his vision inward. But he cheated; he peered out of the corners. He became trapped in detail: why did some women whistle while they walked; why did people have to touch their bodies surreptitiously; why did most policemen look like furniture? He noticed with some surprise that the suits men wore were cut very much like his own. He noticed also that his own suit badly needed pressing. Other people were occupying his thoughts and he had no time for himself. The question was no longer where he wanted to go. He must go forward because he had lost the way back.

But in what condition was he for the journey? His eyes sank into hollows; his hair came loose in his comb. He was not perfect; he was not beautiful; he was now only handsome — and that, a dissolute handsomeness. His eyes, staring permanently outward, wore an uneasy look. If he were going to make contact he had better do it quickly, while some semblance of his looks remained. Having only one direction in which to go, he wanted to get there still in a position to discuss terms.

But contact remained beyond him. He was not involved with life; he was involved with his involvement with life. He looked out at the world, but saw the world only after he had seen himself looking. His strong feelings were for the general; he learned to love crowds.

"I feel you crowds," he whispered to himself as he watched from behind a closed window. "I love you U.N. Plaza, I love you pigeons, I love you East River Tugboats." But he could not particularize. His love failed with one person in the crowd, one tree in the park, one pigeon in the Plaza. To love the world meant to love nothing but narrowing his range was equally frustrating.

He wanted to love women but he could not find a method that worked. Rejection didn't help; now with the disappearance of his looks he was rejected often; the only feeling it left him was a fondness for the girl and a revived faith in people. Rejection made him feel too good. It was obviously not enough; he would have to be more than rejected. He would have to be hurt. Hopefully, Harry decided to make a stab at it.

But first another, more immediate crisis had to be solved. With his loss of looks went his source of income. His apartment was forfeited, his clothing redeemed, his checking accounts canceled.

"What can I do?" he asked Phoebe, helplessly.

"I can't help you," she said, looking down at him. "I can't help anybody."

"Suggest something," Harry pleaded.

"Why don't you get a job?"

Harry had never thought of that.

He went through the want ads. Never having done anything, there was nothing for which he was qualified; however, one ad caught his eye.

"Tall graceful yng men to be trained
as dance instructors. Exp not req. Excel
oppty. Kirby Mercer Dance Studios Inc.
Founder of the Mercer-Quiver System."

6.

The big, flat-faced receptionist handed Harry an application form. Her face was a sketch pad for cosmetics. Her eyebrows were two black pencil streaks, her eyes were purple circles with blackened lashes, her cheeks were reddened by a palette knife and her firm red lips seemed to have been glued on before drying.

Harry filled out the application and handed it back to her. "It's blank," the receptionist said; her nails were red blades; they dug into the paper accusingly.

"I haven't done very much," Harry admitted.

"At least list your social security number."

"List what?" asked Harry.

The receptionist stared at him; one of the pencil marks above her eyes rose questioningly. It occurred to Harry that people no longer grinned at him.

He returned to the Kirby Mercer Studios with a social security card and filled out a second application. The receptionist was joking with another applicant who was resting his elbows on her desk, making hand shadows on a sheet of typewriter paper. Harry saw a quick motion of the elbows and heard two grunted giggles.

"Boy, you'll never get this job," he heard the receptionist say. When he handed her his application he saw that her face was crimson.

"What are you staring at, nosy? A free show? You two go through that orange door and wait in the next room."

Harry followed the other man. He was as tall as Harry, broad-shouldered and good-looking. He walked with a side-to-side motion; each step forward sending him in three other directions as well. The two of them sat with four others in a large waiting room with photographs and pictures of Kirby Mercer blotting out the walls: Kirby Mercer dancing with Bernice Oliver in his first starring film, "She-Devils of Broadway"; Kirby Mercer dancing with Dee Dee Fairfax in their wartime series, "Battleships on Parade," "Dance, Marine, Dance" and "Rhythm Goes to Russia" (later retitled for television as "Rhythm Goes to Rome"); and a wall-length photograph of Kirby Mercer in straw hat, loafers and cane, taken from his final film, the film in which he died dancing —"Johnny Happiness." A hidden phonograph piped an orchestral suite into the room: "The Legend of Kirby Mercer," melodies that he had made famous, now symphonically integrated, with the happy beat removed out of respect for the dead. While waiting, Harry browsed through an edition of the *Kirby Mercer Cook* Book, copies of which were spiced around the room.

Eventually an angular, attractive woman entered, looking quite severe. Little lines of tension stood out on her face. She stared at each applicant as if he were the one who put the lines there.

"Stand, please."

The applicants stood. She pointed to the man who was making shadows. "Walk across the room, please." The man slouched out of his chair and, smiling at the woman, shuffled indifferently across the room. Her color rose. "You," she motioned to Harry and pointed at him to follow. Harry walked across the room. The woman inspected the two men side by side.

"The rest of you can go," she said, and, signaling for Harry and the other man to follow, she opened the door to another room.

It was large and mostly empty, there being by way of décor only a number of fold-up chairs, a wall chart and two basketball nets bracketed to posts at either end of the room. Above one of the nets was the sign: "The Kirby Mercer Basketball System." The sign above the wall chart read "The Mercer-Quiver System." A complicated diagram of the human body ran down the chart: sections were circled, arrows were drawn, blocks of color were laid in. The woman picked up a dangerous-looking pointer and brought it down on the chart with a loud slap. The pointer rested dead center on the body. "My name is Miss Brill." She pointed. She slid the pointer up an inch, leaving a gray scar on the diagram.

"I will be your instructor in the Mercer-Quiver System Method. A scientific approach to physical culture and social dancing. It is true, is it not, that neither of you boys can dance?"

The two men nodded. Harry tried to listen carefully.

"It is easier to teach the Mercer-Quiver System to non-dancers than to have to break dancers of their old habits and retrain them.

"If you will observe the chart, you will see the human body."

"Damn right," grinned Harry's companion. Miss Brill's pointer dipped and rose dangerously.

"As you may observe," she continued, "the diagram is broken down structurally into fifteen separate units. These are known as the fifteen basic quiver units. There are in addition to the fifteen basic quiver units, thirty-five corollary quiver units, but at this point it would be premature to concern ourselves with them."

Harry agreed. It all sounded fascinating.

"Each quiver unit has a life of its own and can gyrate or quiver at will. A quiver as defined by the Mercer-Quiver System is a series of one or more independent or interdependent muscular revolutions occurring at various strategic parts of the body via a self-induced, auto-regulated method of control. A quiver-reverse, which is a slightly more advanced technique, is a series of one or more reverse muscular revolutions stemming however from the self-same quiver control center as the quiver itself."

Harry tried to look interested. His mind was beginning to wander.

"During this period of instruction, the Mercer-Quiver System teaches the student to operate all basic quiver units independently and interdependently. Once the student has mastered his basic quiver unit control he is then ready to learn to dance. It will be your job to teach him."

Teach? Teach what? Harry couldn't remember a thing.

"All Mercer-Quiver System dance instructors are expert in all quiver method dance steps. These include: 'The Mercer,' 'The Grapple,' 'The Conceit,' 'The Harass,' 'The Breach,' 'The Reproach,' 'The Release,' and 'The Quiver!' All of these steps except 'The Quiver' require a partner. 'The Quiver' may be danced with or without a partner, and actually in its purest form is best done alone. Observe."

Miss Brill rested her pointer against the wall and proceeded to demonstrate. Her head shot back at a beat, her eyes disappeared in their sockets, her shoulders dropped away to the sound of finger snaps, her pelvis socked in and out like a plunger, her long legs rubbed up and down each other in quick spasmatic rhythm, a groan let loose from her belly and her dress changed color in front of them. She came out of the dance with a look of beauty and innocence. Her face was sleek with perspiration. Harry fell in love on the spot.

"The Mercer-Quiver System," she resumed lazily, "has in addition to dance instruction proved valuable in weight control and loss of nervous" — she yawned — "tension. Mercer-Quiver offers the students a six-week 'Beginner's Course,' a twelve-week 'Foundation Course,' a twenty-six-week 'Advanced Course' and an eighty-six-week 'Professional Course!'

"As instructors in the Mercer-Quiver System it will be your job to interest the student in subscribing to as beneficial a program as possible. The eighty-six-weeker is the student we can do the most with."

Harry stared into Claire Brill's shining eyes and saw contact there. Love! He knew it at last; he was in love! He waited until the end of the first day's instruction to approach her.

"You know what's happened, don't you?" he said, grinning happily. "I'll meet you outside as soon as I change!"

The shine died in Claire Brill's eyes, "Social contact between supervisory personnel and student instructors is strictly forbidden." She walked coolly away, swaying her fifteen basic quiver units. Harry counted them hungrily. It wasn't really a rejection, he decided. She was only following company rules. He felt confident that it would be no serious problem to find a way around them. He would use his charm.

During lessons he watched the sections of her body click on and off like lights in a house. He tried to imitate the action, follow the clicks to their source, but he had trouble learning. His body was too intent on her body to absorb the rules. Quiver control escaped him; he'd think he'd have it, he'd feel it coming, he'd close his eyes, he'd wait — and nothing happened.

"Quiver! For Christsakes, quiver!" Claire Brill cried out in frustration.

"Show me again," Harry invited, using his charm.

But each demonstration only sank him more deeply into love. He was incapable of the minimal concentration required to register a single decent quiver.

"You're hopeless," said Claire Brill, and began spending more of her time with the other trainee, Guy Peck. Peck was a fast student; Claire Brill quivered and Peck quivered quickly after her. From quiver unit to quiver unit she taught and he followed till a rising rhythm was established between them.

"Unit Fifteen," called out Claire Brill.

"Unit Fifteen," responded Guy Peck.

"Unit Seven," called out Claire Brill.

"Unit Seven," responded Guy Peck.

"Unit Nine."

"Unit Nine."

"Unit Four."

"Unit Four."

"Five."

"Five."

"Three, One, and Two!"

"Three, One, and Two!"

"Thirteen, Fourteen, Six, and One!"

"Thirteen, Fourteen, Six, and One!"

"Seven, Eleven, Twelve, and Three!"

"Seven, Eleven, Twelve, and Three!"

"Units One through Ten," Claire Brill keened.

"One through Ten," gasped Guy Peck, his quiver units beating like a band of pulses. The room shook with their vibration.

"Rest!" Claire Brill cried, and dropped to the floor. Guy Peck dropped beside her. They stretched out panting heavily, a low rumble sounding in their stomachs, gurgling through them till it burst out: wild, intimate, sweaty laughter. Their bodies trembled across the floor. "Want to see my sixteenth basic quiver unit?" gasped Guy Peck. He rose to one knee and made an obscene body gesture. Claire Brill laughed herself against him. Small clouds of dust settled in the air as they hysterically rolled across the unswept dance floor. Harry felt out of things.

He had always been the center; the center outside of whom all others stood waiting. Now it was he who stood outside and the center was Claire Brill. Each day she became more special, more beautiful; each day Harry felt a little further outside. Within her circle were Guy Peck and the receptionist, Florence Chrome. During rest periods the insinuating murmur of Peck's voice echoed from the corner where he staged his anecdotes across to the corner where Harry practiced, with little progress, the art of quiver control. How much easier it would have been to charm Claire Brill if his infatuation hadn't caused him to lose the feeling of his body. Love drove him to fight his own muscles; love cramped his arms and legs with overuse; love put the wrong words in his mouth and robbed him of the opportunity to say even those. Before, he had been filled with emptiness; now he was filled with love. He found that the two emotions were not altogether at variance. Guy Peck, without feeling love, was making out like a thief; Harry, immersed in a sea of the stuff, barely dared whisper for fear of making waves. Love, he now saw, was an obstacle that got in the way of lovemaking.

Still, he was confident that it was only a matter of time until he regained his stride. He composed himself with this knowledge, allowing it to drown out the echoing sound in the corner of Peck's voice outdistancing him. There were those moments when Claire Brill looked Harry's way and gave him his chance to stare warmly, inviting her with the sweep of his eyes to detach herself from the group and join him in what would be their corner. When she did not respond, Harry exercised his way over and loitered on the periphery of their circle. Guy Peck stepped aside and made room for him. Peck called him "Har'" and was very friendly.

"No kidding, Har', you're not a bad-looking guy. You should make out," Peck told him at the end of a day's class.

"Don't worry about me," smiled Harry knowingly.

"Sure, sure, Har'. The girls are crazy for you. I know. It's only that you walk around too much like a dreamer. You know what I mean?"

"Don't worry about me," smiled Harry knowingly.

"You got to do more with your personality. You're too shy. Girls like to be *pushed around*. I knew a girl once who said she *hated* to be pushed around. She pushed around everybody but she hated it for herself. *I* came along and didn't let her push me around. I pushed *her* around. She never got over me.

"You know any dirty jokes, Har'?"

"A few," smiled Harry knowingly.

"The quickest way to make it with a girl is a lot of dirty jokes. Don't stop telling them. She says, 'Stop, stop' — you go on telling them. First she gets mad, then she blushes — then she starts to get *hot*. There's nothing like a lot of dirty jokes to work a girl up to the point you can love her, Har'."

"I have my own methods," smiled Harry.

Peck squeezed Harry's arm reassuringly. "Listen, why don't you take out Florence Chrome from the office ? You can practice on her. She's a good-hearted kid."

Harry smiled.

"Listen, we could double-date. Me and Claire. You and Florence. Why not?"

Harry stared blankly; it didn't register.

"I hate to go out the first time with a girl alone," Peck elaborated. "It gets too complicated, too serious. I run out of material." He paused and squeezed Harry's arm reassuringly. "So it's a date. Right, Har'?" He looked warmly into Harry's eyes and said, "I'd appreciate it, Har'." At which point Harry fell in love with him.

Love wasn't a happening; it was a state, a condition, a porous vessel filling and emptying, filling and emptying. Claire Brill poured into the vessel, Guy Peck tumbled after — and who could be certain there wasn't room for more?

Peck grinned toothily at Harry. Harry, who had never used a toothy grin, grinned toothily back. "Will you be my friend?"

"Asshole buddies, Har'. What do you say?"

"Anything for an asshole buddy," Harry said, sounding very much like Guy Peck.

Peck laughed agreeably. Harry laughed agreeably. They walked down the street looking like twins. Peck taught him some dirty jokes.

Friends.

Harry disappeared; vanished into himself like an inverted stocking; turned inside out to become Guy Peck. He listened to Peck with wonder: what a man! He parroted his voice, his rolling gait, his sense of humor. He tried Peck's dirty jokes in class with Claire Brill, but his imitation failed; he was clumsy. He fumbled punch lines, lost his timing and, twice, had to let Claire finish the stories for him. She did so with great hauteur. Harry got the message; he was not Guy Peck. No, he wasn't; but he could be. And he would be. He watched Peck. He studied his technique in storytelling till he, one day, got Claire Brill to laugh.

"That's not bad," she said, with some surprise. But she didn't tell him one of her own as she would have with Peck. He studied Peck's technique at quiver control.

"You're improving," said Claire Brill, again with surprise.

To joke like Peck, to move like Peck, to dress like Peck, to *become* Peck and then to have Peck's love because Peck would have to love Harry if Harry became Peck, and then — once being Peck, and having his love, gaining also the love of Claire Brill who would have to love Peck — any Peck, even Harry's Peck.

"So it's a date," Peck said, his arm on Harry's shoulder. "I and Claire, you and Florence. Right? It's a date?"

"Well, I don't know," said Harry. Florence was an outsider.

"You'll like Florence, Har'. She's a million laughs. Don't let on to Claire but I took her out once. She's perfect for a shy guy like you."

"Well, I don't know."

"See this bruise on my neck? She'll carry you off kicking and scream-ing."

Harry sulked. "I don't want Florence."

"Who do you want, Har'? Pick her out and she's yours. Anyone you want."

Harry bit his lip. "I want Claire."

Guy Peck looked amazed. He squeezed Harry's arm. "Look, Har', you don't want Claire. She's out of your league."

"I want Claire," repeated Harry, studying his hands. He hoped Peck did not think badly of him.

"Look, Har'. You go double with me this once and I promise you once I'm through with her I'll make Claire go out with you."

Harry looked up gratefully. "You'll actually tell her she has to?"

"Why not? No skin off my ass, huh, Har'?"

It turned out that Florence was at least a million laughs. On the drive out to Claire's she ticked off several hundred and Guy Peck ticked off several hundred and they broke each other up. Following each seizure, Peck, whose eyes were not always on the road, straightened the car, reached across Florence's soft front and squeezed Harry's shoulder. "Huh, Har'? What did I' tell you? All right?"

At Claire's house, Guy left Harry and Florence in the car. "We may as well shift to the back," said Harry.

"Three of us can fit in front," said Florence. "There's no reason for both of us to go."

Harry didn't reply.

"They'll be out any second. You'd better move," said Florence. Harry didn't. They sat in silence for a half hour. At last, Peck and Claire Brill came trotting out hand in hand.

"Aren't we awful?" Claire giggled at Florence.

Harry could not breathe; he had never seen anyone look so beautiful.

"Hey, you two! Somebody make room for the chauffeur!" joked Peck. Harry and Florence moved to the back. Florence's laugh average declined considerably.

She regained her stride in the bar, however. The four of them took a table in a booth, Peck squeezing next to Claire on one side, Florence and Harry pressed away from each other on their side.

"What's black and white and red all over?" snapped Florence.

"A newspaper!" screamed Peck. They wept with the fun of it.

They ordered a number of rounds of beer. Harry became conscious of his billowing paunch. Guy Peck drank beer often and had no paunch; Harry determined to learn how he did it. He concentrated on the paunch, feeling certain that it was the sight of it that turned the perceptive Claire away from him. Like Eugenie, she was hypersensitive; she could no more care for a man with a paunch than Eugenie could care for a man with a pimple on his nose. He would get rid of it, exercise harder, think it away. And, once removed, Claire would see him lean and paunchless and cry, "Oh, Harry. My own Harry!" and they would live to be old together, and Guy Peck would live with them, upstairs, and Harry would tell jokes, many jokes, hilarious jokes, and the three of them would laugh and hold hands across the many years. He ordered another beer.

"I've got one!" cried Claire, "There was this Catholic, this colored guy and this Jew and — wait a minute —" she pondered. "And this Chinaman! And they were all in this lifeboat together —" At the end of the joke Harry roared with the others. He had to have her!

"Your problem, Har'," Guy Peck began to say, but forgot with the movement of Claire Brill's hand beneath the table what Harry's problem was. The lower half of their quiver units wrestled silently under the table.

"What are you doing in there?" grinned Peck, grabbing at an invisible hand.

"In where?" asked Claire.

"Naughty, naughty," beamed Peck and he caught the offending hand and squeezed tight.

"Ouch!" yelled Florence Chrome.

"See, Har', a million laughs! Wasn't I right?" Peck quickly said, and threw himself at Claire's neck before she could open her mouth, "The Werewolf of London strikes at midnight!"

"I'll die!" screamed Claire. "I swear I'll die!"

Harry grinned at her toothily.

"Your problem, Har'," Peck began again.

"Stop it, Guy!" Claire suddenly shouted.

"Your problem, Har'," Peck kept his face turned on Harry while his two arms squirmed under the table, "is that you listen to girls. The idea, I tell you, is not to listen."

"Guy, I mean it!" Claire's face darkened.

Harry grinned at her toothily.

"You see what I mean, Har'?" Guy continued.

"You put your hand up here and the girl says — "

"I swear to God, Guy, you want a slap?" Claire said.

"So you put your hand a little higher and the girl says — "

"You think you're so funny. You're not so funny, Guy. I'm serious !"

"So you go even a little higher and — "

"Guy! Oh, please dear God, make him stop!" Claire quivered.

"Say, listen, Guy —" Harry protested, still grinning. He thought his friend was going too far.

Claire gasped, turned white and then crimson.

"You rat!" she screamed, and threw herself at Guy, giggling shyly. Guy smiled at Harry, very pleased. Claire's head giggled into his protecting shoulder.

"What is it you do again?" Harry asked quietly.

"Don't listen to him, Har'. He's crazy," mumbled Claire from Peck's shoulder.

"Try it, Har'. Florence won't mind. It's an experiment, Florence," Peck assured her. "Put your hand on her knee, Har'."

"Keep your hands off me, Har'," Florence said.

Harry looked hesitant.

"C'mon, Har'! We're separating the men from the boys," Peck said.

Claire guffawed into his shoulder. Peck looked down at her securely hidden head and reached across under the table. He took Harry's hand.

"Don't be afraid, Har.'" He put it on Florence's knee.

"I'll lay you out, Har,'" Florence said.

"See what I mean, Har'! The idea is not to listen," said Peck, his hand pushing Harry's hand up Florence's leg.

"I can't look! I can't look!" screamed Claire, not looking.

Florence, her lips pursed, leaned far over the table. Harry's hand was pushed still higher and then left behind while the other hand explored onward. Florence's heavy lips puckered into a smile. "I mean it, Har' ," she intoned softly, "I really mean it, Har' ."

Claire Brill lifted her head off Peck's shoulder, and Peck drew back. "See how easy it is, Har'?" Harry's hand rested where Peck had left it on Florence's leg. She flicked it off casually and shook with silent laughter. Harry's hand tingled with feeling; he felt the shock waves of Florence's large body vibrating against him. He dared not look at her because if he did he knew that her beauty would blind him; he would never have seen anyone look quite so beautiful.

He took Florence home and they trembled through their coats at each other. Here at last was love, real love: he opening to her; she opening to him. He kissed her large pliant mouth and felt her lips all over his; sucking away Claire Brill, swallowing Guy Peck, covering his body like a poultice. Here was completion; here was oneness; here was *giving!* He did not need to be hurt to feel; he was feeling now. Florence drew Harry's face away.

"Are we going to do this again?" she asked.

"Always," Harry said softly.

"Or do you want to come in and get everything over with tonight ?"

"Tonight. Tomorrow night. What do we care?" Harry asked happily.

"Oh, does Guy want to do it again tomorrow?" she asked.

"What do we care about Guy?" cried Harry ecstatically.

Florence freed her body. "Look, you're a little overexcited now. Tell me at the office Monday when Guy wants to do it again. O.K.?"

"But I want to see you tomorrow," Harry said.

"Only with Guy," Florence said.

"But I want to marry you!" croaked Harry.

"Only with Guy."

Out on the street Harry saw a crowd standing around an ambulance. He waited in the cold for an hour trying to find out what happened and then, remembering the fact of his desolation, he struggled home. In the elevator mirror he saw that the rest of his hair had fallen out.

So this was what it meant to be hurt. Love had been with him, betrayed him and run away. The hollow ghost of love stood in its place, breathing its emptiness before him.

Bald, pimpled, paunchy, hollow-eyed Harry went in to work on Monday and was immediately called aside by Miss Brill, who informed him that the Mercer-Quiver System no longer required his services. A very ordinary-looking girl, thought Harry.

"It's your own fault, Har'," Guy Peck told him. "You really let yourself go to hell." He playfully punched Harry's gut.

"Maybe we can go out sometime together again, Guy," Harry said hopefully.

"You know the way it is with jobs, Har'. People leave and you lose touch." Peck playfully slapped Harry's cheek.

Harry sucked his hurt like a bruise. His head drooped; his shoulders sagged. He limped to the outer office to say goodbye to Florence. How could she resist his broken soul? A girl like Florence couldn't. A girl like Florence would rise like a phoenix from the cold ashes of his hurt, take him in her broad arms, and say, "There, there, Har'. There, there."

"I've been fired, Florence," he said to the girl behind the receptionist's desk. The hurt in his voice shriveled the room.

"Florence isn't in today," said the girl behind the desk. "I think she'll be in tomorrow." Harry fled from the Kirby Mercer Dance Studios.

7.

There was no further use pretending. He couldn't love, he couldn't be hurt, he couldn't communicate, he couldn't make contact, he couldn't do anything. He was a fake! "Maybe I should fingerprint the girls I fall in love with so I'll be sure I'll know them next time!" he cruelly told himself. He was a fake.

But he wasn't alone. He saw pretense everywhere. Life registered on him like a stamp; an overhead hypocrisy thickened his nose; a stare of smugness puffed his eyes; a glare of hostility acned his complexion. Lies, personal and impersonal, further bloated his belly; inconsistency rounded his shoulders; indifference gave him a hacking cough. Little things, normal as street noise, left marks on his consciousness: suits disguising the bodies that wore them; the eerie odor of mass cosmetics; the faces of the aging glamorous, their surplus skin drawn taut with clips secured beneath their bulky wigs. His teeth yellowed. His chin dropped away. His adam's apple stuck out like a pointing finger. The finger pointed inward, caught in his gullet and cried, "Fake!"

He was a romantic fake. A woman who stared at him briefly and walked by became his goddess. Her disdain shone in his eyes like a beacon of eternal worthiness. He had a goddess of the week; dream relationships with ladies who walked quickly by. Their inadequacies blurred into adequacy and their adequacy turned into perfection.

They and no one else were perfect. Harry tried to find them again; looked everywhere; thrilled when the back of a head looked familiar; dropped into deep depression when he saw it was the wrong head; despaired for days until another woman passed, stared at him, and lifted his heart to a height he was sure it would never reach again. Up and down that heart went. He pretended to love, knew he pretended, but continued to pretend anyway. What better emotion was there for him? He let his dreams go high, go low and go high again; shortening the loop so they went faster; not full-length any more, but shorthand fantasies: a beginning cut to middle, cut to end, cut to new beginning. The action whirled, the machine reeled and broke down. Harry was alone with himself again. There was nothing to get in the way of that terrible message: he was a fake.

He was a broke fake. He scarcely had money for food. He could not afford a laundry so he washed and ironed his two remaining suits. They shrank in the wash and Harry shrank to fit them. His nose turned red. Faint networks of blue veins traced across his cheeks, his forehead and his luminescent nose. He picked up odd jobs. He was fired from most of them. Those that did not fire him he assumed were going to, so after the first few days he left them. He scraped enough together to afford a room, sufficient food and, for those moments when his mind ran on unwillingly, a bottle of wine, to slow it. More than anything he wanted to lose the world and be one again. He wanted in; not out. But he found himself chiding little boys not to choke their dogs on the leash, warning vagrant garbage pickers about germs, giving nuns his seat on the subway, helping blind men home.

His soul was wide open. Light, blinding in its unpleasantness, threw deep shadows off the people he watched in the street. He saw, without wanting to, their pride, their cleverness, their pettiness, their confusion, their weaknesses. He placed no value on it; there were too many to choose from. The glare of a traffic light tear-stained his eyes. The whistle of a cop scraped against the walls of his ears. People stared at him and quickened their pace. Harry stared back and knew their histories.

But his knowledge was more than was bearable. He had learned nothing from experience. He had no strength to draw upon. Rather than absorb insights he tried to deflect them off his surface. He saw them coming, and turned away as they smashed against him, scattering through the pores of his body. Their powdered grains pitted his face. One-celled? He had more cells than anybody.

One night he got drunk. He remembered staggering down the street, blissfully bumping passersby. He remembered buttonholing strangers and singing in their faces: "You always hurt the one you love, the one you shouldn't hurt at all." He remembered explaining to a fascinated group of department store pickets that they must learn to give, give, give — or die. Then he remembered nothing again until he found himself sober, staring at the heavily thonged feet of Phoebe Tigerman and hearing her explain to the dozen or so people who sat at them: "Society has no time for people it cannot make use of. Opportunism is its one real value; all economics, religions, and politics are heirs to that value. To put yourself into the business of using or being used is to put yourself into life. To withdraw from that business is to leave life."

Harry swiveled his head and saw Phoebe's well-dressed guests examining him. Their eyes clicked disapproval. Harry turned to Phoebe. She was staring into herself.

"You see?" Harry said, "I *am* being used."

One day, out of money and seeking work, he heard his name not only called but trilled with pleasure: "Haaarrree." It was Belle Mankis.

"You're looking wonderful," she beamed.

"I'm looking for work," Harry mumbled and began to move on.

Belle's face brightened with inspiration. "Come with me. I'll find you work!"

She took his arm and brought him to the Blue Belles.

"You'll never guess who I have here!"

"Haaarrreee," they trilled with pleasure. They passed him from hand to hand.

"He needs money," Belle said.

"We'll give you all the money you want," said India Anderbull, hugging him to her and passing him on to Viola Strife.

"Just stay here with us," said Viola Strife, squeezing him warmly and passing him to Naomi Peel.

"We'll feed you. We'll keep you. We'll take good care of you," said Naomi Peel, passing him on.

"You don't understand," said Harry. "I can't satisfy you. I'm not able to do anything any more."

"Even *better!*" sang the Blue Belles.

In the three weeks they kept him Harry fell in love with them all. They were saintly women; goddesses. He dreamed of marrying and finding happiness with each one in turn. He loved the games they involved him in; he loved being the butt; he loved being laughed at; he loved the attention.

After the third week, the Blue Belles, bloated with revenge and contentment, turned their attention momentarily from themselves and noticed, with shock, the gleam of satisfaction in Harry's face and the beginning flicker of self-interest dancing in his eyes. They threw him out in the street.

It cured Harry of his need for goddesses. He didn't need anything any more. He felt the triumph of simultaneous contact and detachment. Now, with clear, burning eyes he saw all of life at the very moment he was furthest apart from it. It was some kind of trick; a mirage; the closer he came the more distant were his feelings toward himself. He felt everything except Harry. The people he stared at now contained more of him than he did. His left over body puckered like a shriveling balloon. He became smaller as he walked.

One morning he awoke and was completely ugly. No semblance of Harry remained; he was another person. And he was hated. Waves of hate beat at the air he breathed. He smelled its secretion oozing out of the flesh of those who once knew him: revulsion, disgust, contempt. He carried it on his person and where he walked it spread like an epidemic, leaving him untouched as its carrier. He was unpleasant to be near. He no longer looked right. He made people uncomfortable. The uglier he became, the more he saw; the more he saw, the more his judges felt themselves being judged. They hated him all the more for it.

But he did not judge. He could not. He could see but he could not touch. He could feel but he could not react. One day McCandless passed by arm in arm with Stanley Grace. Harry saw them look quickly away.

"The final triumph of White Anglo-Saxon America," he heard McCandless say scornfully. They laughed loudly so that Harry could hear.

Harry tried to hate but he could not. He worked on plans for hate, constructing intricate foundations that collapsed as soon as he tried to build on them. He could not give hate. He could not give love. It seemed pointless to continue experimenting to find out what other feelings he could not give. He decided to die.

8.

He would die blankly. He would die uselessly. He would die, unlike Georgette, for no instructive purpose. But he would die publicly. He would die before a mob. If he couldn't give anything else he would at least give satisfaction. He went to a drugstore.

It was lunch hour. The store was crowded. Its three glass doors flapped in and out; blasts of automobile exhaust came in, blasts of perfumed deodorant went out. "Good afternoon!" said an amplified voice. "Today's specials are —"

A gelatinous mass of aisle wanderers slid past each other, pricing and feeling the specials. Harry entered the tide, breaking into an oncoming swell as shoppers hastily twisted out of his way. He waited in line at the drug counter, selecting from the stacks of decongestants and cold remedies, a common variety of aspirin. Then he waited in line at the lunch counter.

"The Breathing Betty Baby Doll," said the amplifier, "Special today. Actually breathes. Listen to the sound of the Breathing Betty breathe." Gasps of breath shot through the store. "Only $9.95," said the amplifier.

A wide-hipped young woman squeezed off a stool and Harry took her place and waited for service. The customers on either side of him leaned away. The customers waiting for Harry's seat stood well behind him. Harry ordered three Coca Colas. The waitress lined them up on the counter, punched a check and left it, getting wet, beside the Cokes. Harry took two aspirins with each swallow. At the end of the bottle he still felt normal. He took the check and left his stool hearing the murmured mumbles of relief from people at the counter.

"Good afternoon!" said the amplifier.

Harry waited till he got the attention of the druggist and ordered another bottle of aspirin. On the way back to the lunch counter he banged into a revolving rack of paper backs and sent it spinning. The browsers followed the rack around trying to find their places.

Harry waited patiently in line till he found himself another stool, this time from a fat man who quaffed the remains of his coffee with an eye nervously fixed on Harry. He left his wet napkin on the seat. Harry sat on it and waited for service. He ordered three Coca-Colas. The waitress lined them up and left a wet check. "I've only got two hands," she said to the woman next to Harry who had asked for a check, and with her wet hands served a wet sandwich to the man on the other side of him. The scent and clatter of lunchtime trade draped the counter like a mist. "I've only got two hands," Harry's waitress said to somebody near him who asked for a glass of water. No one noticed when he finished his second bottle of aspirin. Near his seat rose the smell of stale soda. "Listen to the sound of Betty breathe," said the amplifier. "Huuhh. Ahuuuhhh. Huuhh. Ahuuuhhh."

Harry waited for the pharmacist to complete the sale of an alarm clock and then he ordered a third bottle of aspirin. A heavily powdered woman knocked over a tray of cosmetics. It bounced past Harry spraying "Persian melon," "Cherries-in-the-snow," "Butterfly pink." The woman glared at Harry as if he had done it. When Harry failed to pick up the cosmetics the woman shook her head and exchanged glances with the pharmacist. Contempt became one of the smells in the store. People deliberately walked in front of Harry in order to stare away from him. He felt a faint dizziness as he waited in line for a stool; but the feeling left as soon as he was seated.

"Three Coca-Colas," Harry said to the waitress, who was getting annoyed. She waited on three other people before lining up Harry's Cokes. "I've only got two hands," she explained to Harry, who said nothing. The lady next to him turned away and began polishing her fork and knife with a napkin. Thinking this last bottle might do, Harry felt around in his pocket for change. He left whatever he found on the counter to cover the cost of his drinks. He wanted to die giving.

He poured out the aspirin. Several missed his hand and burst like popcorn across the counter. "Hey!" he heard people say angrily. It was the last sound from the outside he heard.

His ears suddenly twitched to the far-off sound of himself. It was dim but if he stayed very quiet he could hear it. A half dozen aspirins brought it closer. He heard the real Harry! The sound filled his head with its singular hum. Harry listened, trying to get his body in tune with it. It remained evasive. Other sounds competed with it. "Quiet," Harry commanded the outside world. The lunch counter fell silent, the amplifier died. An ancient memory flickered: Harry, the center, Harry the focus of everyone's life. But it held no more importance for him now than it did then. All that was important was that his eyes had turned inward and he saw Harry.

Harry looked at Harry and saw that he was neither beautiful nor ugly, but perfect. He lifted the final handful of aspirins to his mouth and every hand in the store lifted in silent imitation. He swallowed the last Coca-Cola. The raising and lowering of his arm was like a baton for the craning and settling of dozens of necks. He rose from his stool and the store rose with him. He was one and they were part of his one. He walked harmlessly to the street through a red sea of onlookers.

The store followed him. The street followed him. He sucked up life as he walked, leaving the sidewalks empty. It wasn't love that followed him. There was no love. It wasn't hate that followed him. There was no hate either. It was himself that followed him. The sound of Harry left his head and emptied the world in its cradle. And why shouldn't he be able to feel for everybody? He was everybody. When he was empty, the world was empty; when he was full the world was full; when he triumphed, everybody triumphed; and when he died, the world died.

Then Harry died.